F.R.E.E

Finally Released to Experience Expansion

ALEXIS LIOR

Copyright © 2011 Alexis Lior
All rights reserved.

ISBN: 1463566433
ISBN-13: 9781463566432

This book is dedicated to the beauty of my struggles, which led to triumph and everyone that contributed along the way.

Acknowledgements

First and foremost I would like to thank my father, my friend, my strength, my God. Through this experience I have learned to trust you more than I trust myself. I am so grateful for the opportunity to give my life back to you and accomplish your will for me. If I had a thousand life times, I would live them all for you.

Thanks to my mom Angela Peterson. You are my rock and I truly love you more than words can describe. Thank you for your continual support, love and words of encouragement. They mean the world to me. In my adulthood, we have become great friends and if I could know only one person in eternity, it would be you. Love you Mom.

Many thanks to my brother Jonathan, your wisdom surpasses your years on earth. I love you and there is nothing you can do to make me stop loving you. I know God is going to use your life experiences to leave a legacy on the earth that can not be erased.

To Essence and Janiyah: I do this for you. I believe that ANYTHING is possible and the sky is the limit for you. Tee-Tee loves you very much. Tonya, it has been a journey watching you grow and I know it will only get better.

To my Psuche Achowth (sister of my soul), L.Celest Dunn: Lord, if we're not pure gold by now, I'm not sure when it's coming! Thank you for your prayers, words of encouragement, beautiful spirit and your willingness to come be with me wherever I am in the world. I love you so much and thank God for the wonderful exploits he is doing in your life.

What would I do without my New York homie?! Marlena Burroughs thanks for your friendship, love and support. It is such a joy to watch you follow your dreams. F.R.E.E is finally here!

Kadisha Phelps, who would have ever thought our friendship would lead us here! It has been such a joy to watch you grow. You are truly extraordinary and I thank God for our ever growing friendship. Through the ups and downs, you have seen it all with me and I know we will face the rising sun together. Thanks for always being a friend, love you lots.

Special Thanks to Pastor Craig L. Oliver and the Elizabeth Baptist Church family, I have definitely found the R.E.A.List church this side of heaven. A very special thanks to EBC's Wings of Gabriel, Second Job did it!!! Thanks for your love, prayers, support and always believing in me. Marquis Sterling (Davis), Nicole Lester, Towanda Harris, Keta Anderson, and Retrice Walker thanks for being there to watch me grow. I truly admire you.

MsNickee of Diva Day International, thank you so much for your friendship, love and support. You have truly contributed to the woman I am today. Stay fabulous always.

Thanks to my Atlanta crew: Johnnie Green, Tiffany Flores, Keith Harris (my big brother), Sean Elkins (we are going to take that trip first class!), Kat Cochrane (and dear Rachael) Ms. Flowers, El Medinah, Theron Mintor, Acie Crockett of the ACTODAY Foundation, Lucy Hall-Gainer of Mary Hall Freedom House, Kendra Norman Bellamy and the M-Pact Writers Group. Without your influence I could not have brought this dream to life.

Thanks to my Jacksonville (DUVAL) crew: Raychanda Sellers, Tia Leathers, Jermaine Jackson, Aunt L (Lauretta

Hansberry-Mims), Chloe Mims, the Stewart family, the Peterson family and the best Senior Class Raines has ever seen, Class of 1999. You all are priceless, Ichi Ban. Thank you for always making home feel like home.

To every English teacher I ever had especially Ms. Kelly Ranch and Mrs. Lona Young-Johnson, little Alexis did it! Mrs. Young-Johnson I didn't believe the hype. Thanks for believing in me before I believed in myself.

Sincerest thanks to my editor, Emily Youree. Thank you for your integrity and honesty. This project would not have been the same without you.

To everyone else that I did not mention, please charge it to my head and not my heart.

"Live New, Live F.R.E.E"

Table of Contents

Ch. 1 Introduction: Understanding F.R.E.Edom	1
Ch. 2 Finally: A Moment of Change	5
Ch. 3 Finally: Points from a Powerful Perspective	21
Ch. 4 Released: Destined to be F.R.E.E	31
Ch. 5 Released: From the Pit to the Palace	51
Ch. 6 Experience: Life's Puzzle Pieces	63
Ch. 7 Experience: The Lesson Within	75
Ch. 8 Expansion: Welcome to Destiny	89
Ch. 9 Expansion: The Seven Benefits of Expansion	109
Ch. 10 Live New, Live F.R.E.E	131
Epilogue	143
Study Guide for Chapters 1-10	144

1

Introduction
Understanding F.R.E.Edom

What does the word *freedom* mean to you? In *F.R.E.E* you will discover how freedom can revolutionize your thought process ultimately impacting your life. The beginning letters of this powerful word are *F-R-E-E*. Each letter represents a word that sets the foundation for living a purpose filled, expansive and effective life. The power behind *F-R-E-E* is the ability to view life experiences as stepping stones to your God-given purpose. This method of perception allows you to view the big picture of your life and gain an understanding of where you are destined to go.

The first letter, "F" stands for Finally, which encompasses a moment of realization. When a Finally moment is present, it initiates a seeking process for purpose-driven living. It is also a time when one desires to be enlightened. You may find yourself asking questions like, why am I here? What is my purpose for living?

During this time, answers to these questions are critical and one begins to seek guidance and direction to find purpose.

"R" represents Release. This is a time of relinquishing people, habits and situations from your life. It can also be a time when others release you from their lives as well. Release moments foster many emotions because people, situations, and things that were once stable do not appear to be that way anymore. These chapters will cover the ups and downs of Release, how to handle it and what lies on the horizon when you find yourself in a moment of Release.

Next is "E" which constitutes Experience. Experience is a time to evaluate what is happening in life and begin to ask the question, "What?" This question is not posed to simply receive an answer, but to discover that there is more behind the experience than just going through it. Taking a look at the past will allow you to discover how the events of your life are linked to the purpose and destiny of the future. You will look at how the experiences you journey through fit together to form the "big picture" of life. Through experiences valuable lessons are learned that can be utilized for passionate, purpose driven living.

Lastly, the final letter "E" represents a Promise Land called Expansion. This is where growth meets action and you begin to operate in true purpose. Expansion is the point of combining Finally, Release and Experience and utilizing the lessons from these moments to maximize purpose. At the Expansion level, bondage is non-existent, there is nothing holding you from realizing and reaching your full potential. You will discover the Seven Benefits of Expansion and learn practical ways to continually live the expanded life.

Together, *F.R.E.E* represents Finally Released to Experience Expansion. Learning lessons, maximizing monumental experiences and growing as a result of those lessons are what being *F.R.E.E* is all about. One of the most important discoveries is realizing that moments of life have been orchestrated to create unique lessons that God desires you to learn. There is not one event of your life that takes place by chance. Each experience and life event is linked to you finding and living out an important aspect of your life. The more this viewpoint is applied to your life, the more meaningful each experience will become.

In *Finally Released to Experience Expansion (F.R.E.E)*, the following questions will be addressed.
- What is the lesson in this experience?
- What does it mean to transition?
- How does it all fit together?

Life is the subject of discover; so take the time to make this very real and personal journey.

My hope is that you find yourself within the pages and as a result begin to look at life through the lens of vast proportion.

In the overall picture you will see that God is skillfully placing together something amazing for your life.

In the overall picture you will see that God is skillfully placing together something amazing for your life. By the end of this book, you may be asking yourself some very introspective questions. My prayer is that you turn to God, the author and finisher of all things for the answers. He created your life and it is greatly beneficial to rely on him for the answers to life's tough questions.

As you read, open your heart and your mind. The more you are receptive to what is shared and how it applies to your life, the more you will benefit from it. Allowing God to minister to you is a very important part of this journey. When there is a willingness to listen, his voice can be heard. Allow your spirit to commune with his during your journey and you will surely acquire the F.R.E.Edom that readily waits for you.

I admonish you to keep two verses of scripture at the forefront of your mind as you read and interact with this book. The first is Romans 8:28 (NIV) "And we know that all things work together for good to them that love God, to them who are called according to his purpose." The second is Jeremiah 29:11 (NIV) " For I know the thoughts that I think toward you, saith the Lord, thoughts of peace, and not of evil, to give you an expected end." These two verses are going to light the pathway to your journey toward being F.R.E.E.

God has a destiny for your life. You are so valuable to Him that he has crafted your existence to be meaningful, purpose filled and impactful to those around you. The journey begins here and now. Let us find that place of victory together, let us be F.R.E.E.

"Live New, Live F.R.E.E"

2

Finally

A Moment of Change

Have you been searching? Are you seeking the meaning and purpose of life? Are you ready to embark on a journey that will lead to destiny? It is time to begin one of the greatest journeys of life, one that will lead to the uncharted, undiscovered terrain of the world's greatest treasure, you. Yes, you.

In life, we will spend time looking for things that bring contentment and lead to fulfilling purpose. Searching for purpose is not unusual. The desire to find purpose comes from the yearning to leave an impression and leave the world a little better simply because we were here. This longing of the human spirit does not have to be some grandiose purpose that impacts millions, but knowing that our lives are beneficial in some capacity is important. As we seek, we find ourselves, our place of usefulness and the reason why we exist.

Everyone is born with purpose, an assignment, a goal that is destined to be reached. Some people know their purpose early in life and devote their time to reaching it and living it out. Others go through different professions, gigs, and obstacles before they find their purpose. Finding purpose takes time. Everyone does not reach an understanding of their God-given purpose at the same time. This is what makes the journey to discovering purpose personal and unique.

Imagine, for a moment, what our world would look like if some of the world's most innovative people had not pursued their purpose. What would have happened if Thomas Edison stopped trying to invent the light bulb? What would have become of the Civil Rights Movement if Martin Luther King decided not to take part? Where will the world be if you do not fulfill the purposeful work you are destined to accomplish? How much different would our lives be? This question and a host of others spark a journey to a place of great purpose, meaning and usefulness. It characterizes the F.R.E.E life.

As we walk through each phase of F.R.E.E, we will discover that there is purpose in the events of our lives.

Some experiences make us stronger; some make us wiser, while others serve as investments into our future.

Some experiences make us stronger; some make us wiser, while others serve as investments into our future. In these events, the lessons for living are found and they serve to make us better along the way.

To see clearly or at least know in which direction to go is a desire that most of us will have at some point in our lives. As we journey, we seek to find those things that will positively lead to destiny and purpose. Living without purpose is aimless. People that believe there is no way for them to change the world drift along the road of life with little to no ambition, drive or vision. A lack of vision will destroy your life. Without knowledge of where you are going; the likelihood to waste time, make multiple mishaps and get off of the designated path is bound to happen.

It does not matter when you begin to search, it only matters that you begin. It is never too late to embark on the road to purpose. If you are at the searching point, this is a great place to begin. If you are not yet there, as you read, you may find yourself relating to what you have been experiencing. Seeking F.R.E.Edom can begin for you as well.

Your life has a purpose. Whether you realize it or not, your journey has already begun. The purpose that you are seeking is already seeking you. You are here because you were appointed to be here. Your life matters. At this moment you can begin to look at your life in a way that you can see the building blocks on the road to liberation. F.R.E.E will serve as the construction material while you journey on this life-changing road.

First Step: Finally

Finally is the first step in the journey to the F.R.E.E life. In order to begin, a step has to be made and this phase is the forerunner of the process.

A Finally moment is a turning point. It is an event, experience, or moment where you say, "Enough is enough". It is a time of enlightenment. Something is stirring, moving, and changing within you; you are viewing your life from a point of awareness based on what you are experiencing.

During a Finally moment, you move from sitting on the sidelines of life to actively participating in it.

During a Finally moment, you move from sitting on the sidelines of life to actively participating in it. Becoming an active participant in the journey of life requires accountability. A Finally moment is a time when you view your past and take a true assessment of it. Being honest with yourself during a Finally moment is key. It allows you to truly acknowledge your past for what it is. As this takes place, you can see how your moments have aligned with an intentional purpose.

Finally is a place of adjustment. You are ready for change. The desire for change provides the fuel for making adjustments. There is a desire for advancement, which is also fuel for change. Advancement is an aspect of growth, which takes place in all things that have life. Growth and development lead to advancement. At the Finally phase, advancement is the desired outcome. As you become better, you will begin to seek a more meaningful life.

Timing and action are correspondents in the Finally stage of becoming F.R.E.E. What happens and when it happens are two very powerful components when it comes to embarking on the

F.R.E.Edom journey. Timing will allow you to seize the moment at the proper time and function in it effectively. When the timing is right, action can take place swiftly and accurately for the maximum effect.

It is important to recognize a Finally moment in your life. When a Finally moment is identified, it becomes easier to classify and view a situation and its circumstances for what they really are. The reality of the moment and finding true value is the goal. The value leads to greatness, which is ultimately where we are destined to be. When we take time to identify the meaning behind a situation, circumstance or moment we identify purpose.

Attributes of Finally

A distinguishing factor of a Finally moment can be found in its beneficial attributes. These attributes occur when the moment has arrived. Recognizing these attributes allow you to understand what you are being presented with and how to take valuable steps toward the F.R.E.E life. The recognizable attributes are: Preparation, Enablement, Awareness and Renewal.

Each one serves as a building block to a greater place and as we see them working in our lives, we begin the journey to liberation.

Preparation for Greatness

When you encounter Finally moments in your life, there is an aspect that precede the moment called preparation. To be prepared means to make ready, to be up to the challenge, to experience those things that condition you for what is coming next. As you are prepared, you encounter situations that you have never experienced before. Aspects of your life change in order to prepare you for where you are going.

Preparedness is a huge advantage. When you are being prepared for greatness and purposeful living you positively gain from life's circumstances instead of simply fumbling through them. You are empowered with the understanding that you are being prepared for greatness, this notion allows you to handle things from that perspective.

In most instances there is preparation period, a time that setting up and staying alert is necessary. Preparation can take place knowingly or unknowingly. To knowingly prepare means that you are intentional about the actions you take. They are taken with a definite reason in mind. To prepare unknowingly means that there are events taking place in your life that are teaching you lessons in order to prepare you for what is coming.

During my Finally moment of professional transition, the preparation came at various times. I began to feel unrest in my profession about a year before the change took place. This was my preparation period. I had a desire to write a book and fulfill my purpose. There was an urge in my heart calling me to become an author regardless of what the circumstances looked like. As I felt this urge to write, I prepared myself by meeting writers, starting a blog and writing consistently in my spare time. These acts of preparation set the wheels in motion and as the Finally moment arrived, I was already prepared for the next part of my journey.

Preparation is extremely important to the experience. God will not allow you to walk through a situation he has not prepared you for. You are prepared in order to fulfill purpose.

If there is a yearning within you for a change or if you are sensing a transition, you are experiencing preparation for something greater. Embrace what is happening to you, pray about it and ask God what to do about what is taking place within you. When you ignore what you are feeling or deny it, you will be unprepared when your Finally moment arrives.

During my time of professional transition, preparation made a major difference in my life. If I would have been unprepared, I would have been overwhelmed by fear and doubt and uncertain in the face of what was happening to me. However, being mentally and spiritually prepared caused me to view the loss as a transition to purpose. I understood that the transition out of that profession was the Finally moment I needed in my life.

Internal preparation takes place in different ways. Each type of preparation is equally important. The three types of preparation are: mental, social and spiritual.

Mental preparation comes through the changing pattern that is occurring in your life. There is a desire to change routines, habits or characteristics about yourself or surroundings that have been part of your normal way of life for years. There is a hunger for change.

During mental preparation the mind questions and wonders. The future plans become a reoccurring thought and they are taken seriously. The mental preparation stage can be overwhelming. Rest assured that the decision to change mentally is a result of a desire to grow and become better.

John 8:31-32 reads: "Do not think as the world thinks, but be transformed by the renewing of your mind." (NIV) When our minds are renewed, the desire to change mentally only comes from the spiritual preparation that is happening within us. We are connected to God by the spirit. The longing for spiritual growth and a change in thinking is a sign that God is preparing you. Allow the Lord to change your mind and submit your heart to his will.

This leads to spiritual preparation. God is drawing you to himself through this form of preparation.

Preparation is a wonderful stage. It means change and growth are on the horizon. As your soul and mind line up with the desire to change, you are stirred for great purpose. The stirring of the spirit is never by accident. It is ordered by God's providence. Do not be afraid of what is happening, allow God to work through you and with you.

The last type of preparation is social preparation. During social preparation, the landscape of your friends, associates and colleagues will begin to change. As you align yourself with purpose, your interests and how you spend your time will change as well. Social preparation is a notion of desiring deeper, more meaningful relationships and connections.

Social preparation is one of the most amazing parts of the transition and one of the most abnormal. People are positioned based on what you need and the next level that you are called to. Divine connections take place when you are being socially prepared to fulfill purpose. It is important to be open to the introduction of beneficial people into your life that can contribute to where you are going.

We are given a promise that we will not receive a situation, burden or circumstance that goes beyond our level of preparedness. What we encounter, we are prepared to handle regardless of how we feel. We are given essential pieces of preparation and the tools to handle it. That is not just in some situations, this fact holds true in all situations. Isn't this a beautiful part of God's plan? Just think, God gave us the tools of preparedness to handle moments of change and transition in life. Wonderful!

Without preparation, confusion and misunderstanding can set in and once this occurs, the reasoning for the Finally can be hard to regain. The journey will not be an easy one, but with Christ all things are possible. This is what he wants us to understand. If it was a situation that we could handle ourselves, why would we need to be prepared? We must view our situation outside of the limitations of our thinking. This requires a God-sized perspective. When we have it, nothing can stand in the way of making the most out of a Finally moment.

Preparation and perception serve as the predecessors to purpose and reason.

Preparation and perception serve as the predecessors to purpose and reason. A positive perspective frees the mind for expansion to take place. Thinking outside of the current situation allows vision and focus to come into play because more is seen than what exactly appears. Preparation enables you to be mentally, spiritually and socially prepared for the journey ahead.

Enabled: Equipped to Win

Understand that the Finally phase is about being empowered through the strength of God. In Isaiah 45, there is a story about King Cyrus. He did not believe in the God of Israel, but he was enabled to free the Israelites on several occasions. God promised that he would smooth out the mountains and cause him to defeat his enemies. God anointed Cyrus for such a time to complete the assigned task and he was enabled to win.

Finally moments bring out the best in us. They show us that we have been equipped to handle whatever we face. In addition we come to realize that God is the source of this enablement. We depend on him to direct our paths and ultimately lead us to F.R.E.Edom. Whether the situation that we are facing is favorable or not, Finally moments have a way of showing what we are really made of.

God has equipped you to withstand a Finally moment. The Finally moment is the beginning of the enabling process, it is a time that really shows what God has placed on the inside of you and it calls you to act and think from this new perspective. He opens your eyes to recognize the moment of transition that leads to a higher place for you. The perspective is what makes the difference in your situation.

With the presentation of a Finally moment, God gives you an opportunity to be enriched with more faith, power and possession to do what you are being called to do.

You are enabled by the Power of God.

You are enabled by the Power of God. This enablement causes you to see the situation from God's perspective. Jeremiah 29:11-13 reads, "For I know the plans I have for you," declares the Lord, "plans to prosper you and not to harm you, plans to give you hope and a future. Then you will call upon me and come and pray to me, and I will listen to you. You will seek me and find me when you seek me with all your heart." (NIV) Seeking God is the answer to becoming enabled during a Finally moment. Once we understand that we are empowered, we can seize the opportunity of the moment. Many people do not realize that they are enabled to win. They believe that they are defeated before they fight and less than victorious when they are promised the victory. You must get to a point where you seek God in everything, both the fortunate and unfortunate moments of life. This is what leads you to F.R.E.Edom.

The Beauty of Awareness

Awareness is the standpoint of knowing that the situation that you are facing will cause transition. The Finally moment that you are experiencing is ultimately leading you to be F.R.E.E. You have a heightened sense of understanding of those things that are occurring around you. When someone is aware, they are alert and insightfully looking at what is in front of them.

This sense of awareness is not meaningless. Awareness is full of purpose and its reasoning is intentional. The Finally moment in your life is hinged on your ability to recognize what is happening.

In the situation of awareness, it will call you to do some unconventional things like changing your habits or breaking free of people. Inside you know these things are necessary in order for the Finally moment to be fully manifested. Knowing what to do with the awareness that you have is very important because it is a turning point for you and others as well. You will select the correct course of action because you are aware of what is happening in and through you.

When you are at the point of awareness, you benefit in the process. You are allowing F.R.E.Edom to take place within you. You must pay attention to the awareness that God is presenting to you. If you see that something is not working in your life and God is allowing you to be aware of it, there is a reason behind this. He is attempting to change something in you. You must utilize this benefit of awareness wisely and allow it to lead you to advancement.

A Life Renewed

Are you tired of your present circumstances? Sick of struggling with situations? Have you ever thought, there has to be a better way of living and existing beyond what is in front of me? If you have ever said these things or even thought them, you are not alone. I have been there and I'm quite sure most of the people you know have been there as well. The last attribute of Finally is renewal.

Renewal is defined as the quality or state of being renewed. It is the rebuilding of a large area and my personal favorite definition: an expenditure that betters an existing fixed asset. These definitions of renewal are different, however, they encompass one similar characteristic. They include advancement. When something is renewed it is being refined and shaped to function more efficiently and purposefully than before.

The definition that speaks about the rebuilding of a large area is a wonderful example known as "urban renewal". In major cities when urban renewal takes places, everything in the area is completely demolished leaving no signs of what previously was. After the old is torn down, the new and improved structures are erected and the area has a new look. The property value of the renewed area is increased and neighborhood is revitalized with new people and businesses.

This example of renewal is amazing because it is literally where the change takes place. This is reminiscent of what happens when there is a Finally in your life. You are given the attribute of renewal. It is the new strength that arises in you; this strength is supernaturally supplied by God to fuel your journey. You are given the strength to endure your Finally moment and it serves as a forerunner to the F.R.E.Edom journey that has been prepared for you. One of my favorite scriptures, Isaiah 40:31 emphasizes this very well: "But they that wait upon the LORD shall renew their strength; they shall mount up with wings as eagles; they shall run, and not be weary; and they shall walk, and not faint." (NIV) This is one of the greatest scriptures on endurance that I have ever read. When you are going through the renewal process, endurance is necessary. This promise is the sure sign that God is with you. As you complete the journey set before you, God will allow you to be renewed and not become worn down in the process. This is a benefit of a Finally and of F.R.E.Edom as a whole. We are given the opportunity to have a complete renewal as a part of our liberation. Finally is the opportunity to seek transitional change and allows us to recognize that we can live a renewed life.

Renewal is a complete process that includes the mind, spirit and body. To be renewed is to embrace change which requires perception to be in order. God has given us an opportunity to experience renewal that will benefit us in the Finally moments of our lives and beyond. Being renewed is an attribute and benefit of being a child of God. When something is renewed, it is refreshed and revived; life is breathed back into it. God has breathed his life on you and chosen you to be F.R.E.E. Utilize your Finally moment as an opportunity to irradiate the old and possess the new.

To Live is To Reflect

In order to fully embrace a Finally moment. You must reflect on what contributed to the arrival of this pivotal time. This may assist with making sense of what you are currently experiencing on your journey. A reflection is simply a look at what was to determine and clarify what will be. In order to turn the corner, write a new chapter or end one for that matter, it starts with a reflection on the past.

We all need a reference point, something to anchor us, remind us and at times inspire us not to return to that place again. To reflect is to glance into the past learning something pivotal along the way and applying the lesson for the purpose of growth. It is useful for gathering strength, wisdom and guidance. It maybe in the form of a family member's words like something your mother or grandfather said or it maybe embracing your own past allowing you to completely let go of an experience and walk in the light of a new day.

A Finally moment does not necessarily have to categorized as one event or experience. It could be a season or a collaboration of things that caused you to get to a turning point of change. The point is that the Finally moment caused something to break and as a result you desire change for the better. You believe this so much in your heart that it propels you to change at any cost. This point can be one that makes you relentless, meaning you are willing to come out of your comfort zone to find the change that resonates deep in your heart.

Finally moments are personal and unique.

Finally moments are personal and unique. The characteristics of your Finally are as intricate as a fingerprint. There maybe similar patterns, but the print is a one of kind design. God cut your Finally from the pattern of your life and is weaving a wonderful garment for you to show the world and it does not look like anything else he has made. Your experiences are unique to you and in order for you to fully embrace your situation and moment you have to accept this uniqueness.

3

Finally

Points from a Powerful Perspective

The Power of Choice

With life situations, there are positive and negative aspects of every situation. During a Finally moment and all of the phases of F.R.E.E, it is beneficial to view circumstances from a positive perspective. It directly affects the way circumstances are handled. If time is spent magnifying the negative in any situation, it will alter your perception and ultimately affect the outcome. This is why it is important to spend time accentuating the positive.

I know you are thinking—You don't know my situation, this is the breaking point of my life. I understand where you are coming from and I empathize with you. There have been moments in my own life when I wanted to throw up my hands and give up in the face of a negative circumstance. I had to remember that everything is working together for the advancement of my life and there is a lesson in every circumstance. Take it from a F.R.E.E veteran, the circumstance you face will produce a better outcome if you decide to view your situation positively from the very beginning.

The decision to have a positive perspective is not always easy to adopt.

There is a conscious choice involved when adopting positive thinking.

There is a conscious choice involved when adopting positive thinking. The notion is to confront what is happening and not deflect it, even if it not desirable. The perspective of your thinking is very important during this phase because it will determine what you receive from the situation as a whole.

When you face a circumstance head on, you deal with the reality of the situation. Dealing with reality will enable you to deal with the facts and accept them for what they really are. When you make a decision to deflect and not deal with the reality of a negative circumstance it can not be properly assessed. Making an assessment of a circumstance is the first step to viewing it from a positive perspective.

We must search below the surface to find the positive attributes in life's circumstances. Romans 8:28 teaches on perception: "And we know that in all things work for the good of those who love him, who have been called according to his purpose." (NIV) God works for the good of those who love him, who have been called according to his purpose."(NIV) This reassurance gives us hope beyond the situations and circumstances of life. God promises to work out all things together for the good. He is in control of our lives. We are called to perceive situations and circumstances in the good light He functions in. Remember, a positive outcome may not always appear on the surface, but it is an ever-present factor because God is working life situations out for your benefit.

Negative and positive thinking are choices that we have the opportunity to make each and every day. We make a choice to think about the situations of our lives in either a beneficial way or one that will cause thoughts of drudgery. In this chapter, we will study both.

Negative Thinking

On life's journey, we will experience bad circumstances. The outcome will not go in a favorable direction and turmoil is inevitable. This is life and it happens to all of us. However, we still have a choice of perspective.

A negative perspective says, "Why, why, why? This isn't what I deserve! I can't believe this is happening at this point in my life!, I CAN'T take this!" This mentality is called panic mode. Panic happens very quickly and it is a perspective where one snapshot of a situation causes an emotional, immediate reaction.

This immediate reaction may not take the entire situation into account.

When I was growing up, my mom would often tell me that I was too calm about things. It seemed as if nothing affected me because my demeanor was one of non-reaction even in the face of something negative. It wasn't that the situation did not affect me; I made a choice not to react immediately.

The choice for immediate reaction is one that may not always lead to the best outcome. There are times when immediate action is necessary like when someone is in trouble in a body of water or someone is going to be injured. However, an initial reaction to a seemingly adverse situation may not be the best response. It is likely that the entire situation is not being considered.

Panic breeds panic. When you are in panic or reaction mode, there is an absence of rational thinking. Panic not only affects your perspective, but those around you making it easy for them to adopt this disposition as well. When you have more than one person panicking in a situation, it is a recipe for drowning in a sea of emotion.

Negative thinking causes a negative reaction. When the mind has already conceived an outcome to a situation the actions that follow convey what we anticipate to happen. For example, when you have been in an argument with someone and it is not fully resolved and then you see him or her for the first time following the encounter, you may display a defensive posture. Even if the person says, "Hi, I bought you lunch to apologize for our argument." The initial reaction might be, "I don't want lunch!" Even though there is an act of reconciliation happening, the outcome has been premeditated by your negative thinking.

Our sense of notion, premeditation, pre-judgment and negative thinking greatly influence how we view a situation.

Thoughts dictate actions.

Thoughts dictate actions. If we think negative initially, the thoughts can be changed, but if the actions that are starting to occur reflect a negative mindset, damage control will have to be performed in order to rectify what has occurred.

Negativity is transferable. Test it. Intentionally spend time with a negative thinking person. Chat with him or her, go to lunch with him or her and interact on purpose. After spending time with him or her, examine your own thoughts, see if anything you say or do reflects something he or she said or did.

The mentality of negatively can spread very quickly. It can be passed along unknowingly and before it is realized the thinking has been adopted. The power of negativity is undeniable; there will be side effects. Keep in mind that a positive or negative perception is a choice.

The power of choice is vital to recognizing a Finally moment. If there is negativity around, do the best you can to avoid it. The action to avoid has to be intentional.

I have found it helpful to make a mental list of the people, things or moments that are sources of negativity and then I am intentionally avoid them.

Don't let your thinking be dictated by negativity. Allowing this perspective to persist will cause you and your experience to suffer. If the source of negativity is coming from within then keep reading! The path to positive thinking is just ahead.

The Power of the Positive

How much would the aspects of your life improve if you had a positive outlook? Could you get out of debt, start a career that you're passionate about, fulfill a dream or vision or step out and share a talent that you have been hiding?

You may feel accomplished, happy, free or relieved just by thinking a positive thought. Dwelling on positive thoughts are followed by good feelings, embracing these feelings is very beneficial. When you think positive thoughts, it allows you to relinquish the negative ones. There is power in positive thoughts because they are progressive. If thinking about the positives of the situations and experience of life is tough, then practice it. Routine thinking is fine. A change of mind must come before there is the desire to act on the feeling. It has to become a habit before it can become a part of your character.

God has enabled us to think positively. In Isaiah 26:3 we are reminded "You keep him in perfect peace whose mind is stayed on you because he trusts in you." (ESV) God allows us to stay positive and peaceful when our minds are kept on him because he is the source of our peace and positive thinking.

One of the most beneficial Finally moment I've had came in the form of unemployment. I know you are thinking "how"? I was praying about a change in my career path, never thinking that God would answer through a transition that caused me to be unemployed for five months. I did not realize completely what was happening; I had a mortgage and other financial responsibilities. Unemployment wasn't necessarily what I had in mind. What was I going to do? In the face of that question, I decided to view the situation as a positive realizing that all loss was not a bad thing.

I had been praying for God to open a door for me to move in the direction of my passion which had nothing to do with my current occupation. I did not want to just quit without knowing where God was leading me to go. I felt that he wanted me to stay in that position until an opportunity was opened. I identified that this was a Finally moment and that everything that occurred up to this point had prepared me for it.

My actions after this point were ones that were fueled by my positive perspective. During the time I was unemployed, most people that knew me well did not know what I was experiencing. My attitude remained positive and many new people were drawn to me. I formed lasting relationships that were beneficial to me long after the Finally situation ended.

The power to think positively causes a change of perception the same way negative thinking does. The difference between positive and negative thinking is that positive thinking keeps looking and searching for faith and hope.

When thinking is positive, the perception is positive and there is an opportunity to see more than what is connected to the experience.

When thinking is positive, the perception is positive and there is an opportunity to see more than what is connected to the experience. This attitude of faith and hope lets you know, this is not the end, this is not all there is—keep searching and the light will come on. As a result the actions connected to a positive attitude yield positive results.

You are empowered when you think positively. Positive thinking reflects in your actions. Pray about thinking positively. God is the author and finisher of our faith. When we take on his positive thoughts about us, his spirit engulfs us and our mentality is enlightened. The choice to think positively will be a great asset to your journey.

The Role of Relationship

Relationships become volatile and necessary as transition occurs. They are meaningful and purposeful in the preparation process because the relationships are strategically designed. The purpose is to gain a lesson out of each relationship. The people that surround you will have an influence on your thinking, the words which are spoken to you and by you are vitally important.

The Word of God says, "Life and death are in the power of the tongue." (Proverbs 18:21a KJV), what you speak and what is spoken to you has power especially during a time of transition.

Be careful to observe those around you and notice how the face of your social circle maybe changing. It is not by chance that change is occurring, God is allowing people to come in and go out for a reason and this reason is one that is contributing to your advancement.

Following God's instructions about who to speak with, confide in, and allow access to you during a Finally moment of your life is key. Be careful to listen and most important, obey the instructions given concerning relationships.

The people that you are being surrounded with are contributing factors to your F.R.E.E journey, their presence is purposeful. People are placed in proximity to you for a reason, observe these interactions very carefully. Finally moments are greatly maximized when we realize the effects of people in our lives.

Finally and the Next Step

Transitioning through a Finally moment is a means by which to get to a better place. It is a turning point, a fresh start, an eye opening experience that is meant for your advancement. It is unique because it impacts your next move, clarifies direction and allows you to focus on what is really important. Experiencing this moment offers a greater understanding into what will happen next and most importantly teaches you valuable life lessons.

The F.R.E.Edom journey is about progression. The next step after the transition of a Finally moment is the progression of the Release. Release comes about because of the events that have occurred in your life. It is a place of what I like to call "delightful difficulty" It is difficult because there is movement from a familiar, comfortable place to a place that is unfamiliar and sometimes equally uncomfortable. The delightful part is that there is newness all around you. This uncharted territory of new moments, people and places to discover are all contributing to God's most treasured creation—YOU.

4

Released

Destined to Be F.R.E.E

Released to Be F.R.E.E

Release is being free of entanglement, bondage, and restraint. It means to let go of that which inhibits. Through letting go, you experience solidarity of the mind and spirit. When solidarity comes there are no limits; thoughts, visions and dreams are endless. After the Finally moment there comes a time to let go of those things that have been holding up our liberation and weighing down our hopes and dreams. You are positioned to relinquish those burdensome things and embrace the new day of growth and change that lies ahead.

Imagine how a bird feels when it leaves captivity. It flaps its wings expediently, elevating quickly as it builds momentum with every flutter. You may even hear the bird begin to sing as it disappears out of sight. As we imagine that bird, we saw the scene in our minds and felt the liberation in the release, realizing that he was headed to a better place. What a joy the free bird must have felt as he realized that days of liberation were before him. The same way this bird was liberated is the same way release comes into our lives.

Release is a great thing. It is a monumental turning point to greatness and an opportunity to listen and see development take place right before your eyes. In order to see this development, there must be an increased level of insight, which includes being optimistic about what is seen. Even if the release does not appear to be a positive thing from the onset, there is still power in what it brings.

We have the ability to view circumstances from different angles. As we do this we see more than what lies on the surface.

How to Recognize a Release Moment

In order to fully benefit from a situation that involves a Release, it is important to know how to recognize it. The Release process comprises two actions: one entity performs the relinquishing and the other is relinquished. At different points, you can be on either side of this spectrum.

Release is a separation from people or things that takes place at any given time for numerous reasons. Circumstances lead to Release, growth leads to Release and change leads to Release just to name a few. Whatever the reasoning is behind the Release, the goal is to discover why the moment is happening and how it relates to your advancement. As individuals we have a tendency to view letting go negatively, but it is not always this way. There is something greater happening when Release is taking place, even if it appears to be negative. Viewing it as beneficial will shed great light on the growth and development you are experiencing.

When someone decides to let go of a bad habit like smoking in exchange for a better lifestyle, that isn't so bad right? Letting go of the habit will require adjustment, but it is a step towards better health. It is the same way with other Releases in our lives. We may not want to walk through it because it is different and if we are letting go or being relinquished it can appear as an undesirable end. Release contributes to the advancement of our F.R.E.Edom.

When a Release is taking place, especially in the realm of relationships, it can cause a range of spiritual, mental and physical affects. It is normal to feel the affects of an absence from your life, whether it is your choice or not. Since there are three parts (spiritual, mental and physical) that make up our being, it is ok to feel the affects in more than one area. Many times these affects take place simultaneously and they range in emotion. When this occurs it is important not to allow emotions or feelings to take control. You can control how you are feeling no matter how painful it is. We have the power through God to take control and make adjustments which will allow us to experience the beauty of life from every aspect.

It is important to recognize when physical, mental and spiritual adjustments are present during moments of Release. One of the greatest examples of this in my life was during the death of my grandmother. My family is small and I was very close to my grandmother. Like most grandparents, she was full of wisdom, and I learned a lot from her. She knew me before I knew myself and I loved her dearly.

While she was in the hospital in another state, I flew and drove back and forth constantly to be with her and my mom. I didn't know when I would see her for the last time, so I cherished the moments that we spent together. Her ordeal in the hospital was very difficult for my family and the hope of recovery was slim. I began to pray about what to do. Slowly and hesitantly, I was mentally and emotionally preparing for her passing. God was allowing me to release her so that I could eventually embrace a valuable lesson in this situation.

My brother said something very profound to me during the last days of her life. He said, "I don't believe Grandma will leave us until she knows that we are okay with letting her go." This has stuck with me from that day forward. God won't allow anyone or anything to be released until there is preparation to handle it. Even if it feels as if we are not ready, God is still our more than enough and he has equipped us from the beginning of time to handle it.

The more I began to realize the truth of Romans 8:28; I saw how it was working for the good of all of us. Without a divine miracle, she could not live in the condition that she was in. She asked my mom and I one day, "When am I going home? I'm ready to leave here." We believe her question was deeper than we realized. She was asking us, but we believe she was really posing the question to God. That was the last time I saw my grandmother alive. Her question was answered in her transition from this life. Reflecting on it brings a variety of emotions out of me, but I understand that her passing was orchestrated and when the time came, it happened as God commanded. I found a great deal of comfort and strength in knowing that it is working together for good and contributing to my (F.R.E.E) life.

During this time of transition for me and my family God knew the outcome from the beginning. Even though it was out of my control, God was in control.

In all Release moments we must recognize the sovereignty of God.

In all Release moments we must recognize the sovereignty of God. "And we know that all things work together for good to them that love God, to them who are the called according to his purpose." Romans 8:28 (NIV) The key is that we must know that whatever is happening, it is working toward a positive result.

The Release Process

Release begins with recognition. Acknowledge a Release for what it is: a letting go process. If you are willing to view it like this, it will contribute to your growth. Release becomes developmental when we ask ourselves fact finding questions like "what does this release mean?" and "how can this be a positive situation for me?" These practical questions are good ways to recognize the Release and become okay with the process. Second, Release is a transitional and progressive process. It is transitional because it has a beginning and an end. Every situation of life is filled with transition. The Release is transitional because like the Finally moment, it is a passing point that possesses some moments of self assessment.

Release is progressive because newness is emerging in your life. You are making strides toward better connections, habits and experiences of life. The Release moments of my life have been some of my most progressive moments. The Release process is a shedding of sorts. There are layers of relationships, habits and experiences that are falling away and new, beautiful relationships, habits and experiences are emerging.

As progression unfolds, we find the beautiful potential that lies on the progressive road. It could not be recognized without Release. Progression characterizes Release and makes direction more visible.

The beneficial elements are seen in the value Release brings to the quality of your life. Although transition is taking place and it feels like you are "shedding", Release is adding something far greater than what you can see.

As we live, we accumulate baggage, scares, wounds and unnecessary burdens along the way. The benefit of a Release is that we can relinquish baggage and press life's reset button. The cycle of holding on to unnecessary things can be crippling. When Release happens the journey becomes easier without the emotional, mental or physical baggage. The Release process allows us to focus on self and invest in adding character to who we are and who we are destined to be.

When Release is occurring in your life, you and the people around you are changing. Let's focus on relationships for a moment. If there is an unexpected break in pattern, routine, thoughts or action of the people in your life it is natural to ask why. You may find yourself not relating to the people or things that once held your attention and interest. You may feel outcast or lonely. These are evident signs a Release taking place in your life.

Release is not a solo act: you are not the only one that has encountered such a thing. Even though it may feel like a solo experience, others have encountered it. As you transition through life, it is likely that you will experience Release more than once. The key to making Release beneficial is learning how to deal with it so that it does not become a place of bondage, but a stepping-stone to living a Finally Released to Experience Expansion (F.R.E.E) life.

As we walk through this chapter, I admonish you to take a look at your life and hold what you have experienced to the light of Release. As you do this, you will begin to embrace the journey that lies before you, allowing it to contribute to your F.R.E.Edom.

Released While Holding onto the Promise

Do you believe that God has a plan for your life? Do you think you were placed on earth to fulfill that plan? God does have a plan and will for each and every one of us. This is the promise found in Ephesians 1:11 "In Him we were also chosen, having been predestined according to the plan of Him who works out everything in conformity with the purpose of His will." (NIV) We are recipients of his promises when we decide to allow our lives to function in accordance with his will.

As we discussed earlier, Release includes a process that involves God orchestrating an occurrence that involves letting go. In this, we accept what God has allowed to happen and find the value in it that contributes to our growth. The second part is where we find F.R.E.Edom because our minds and spirits are renewed by the value that we have extracted from the Release. Release becomes valuable when we look at it in the way that God wants us to see it.

The best way to view Release is through the lens of God's promises.

The best way to view Release is through the lens of God's promises. God's view is shown through His Word time and time again. The second key verse of this book holds a promise that we remember as we walk toward our place of Expansion by way of Release. "For I know the plans I have for you," declares the LORD, "plans to prosper you and not to harm you, plans to give you hope and a future." Jeremiah 29:11 (NIV) I would like you to recognize something very important, let's look at this from the Kings James version: "¹¹For I know the thoughts that I think toward you, saith the LORD, thoughts of peace, and not of evil, to give you an expected end."

God is promising peace and an expected end. He knows what we are facing and what we are encountering during Release. In order to make it to the expected end, we must take God at his Word and trust him without fail. Trust builds faith which leads to action. The activation of faith makes God's Word come alive in our lives. Hold on to the promises that God has spoken regardless of what a Release looks like. Remember it is designed for peace and an expected end.

Viewing life from this perspective means Release is a contributing factor to our growth and development. It enables us to be more effective in dealing with the circumstances and personal affects that are faced. It also positions us to ask for God's help in the process.

The Release is contributing to your life more than you realize. I have recognized this early in my adult life. When I was in my early twenties, I stepped into the WORLD OF WORK. I was a college graduate and it was time to get my FIRST REAL WORLD JOB, which is what most college students like to call it. Paying my own bills, establishing a work history and living independently were my goals of obtaining a start to a career. I got my first "real world job" and stepped into a career field that I loved. I relocated to another state knowing no one at all; I threw myself into my job. The work was difficult, detail-oriented and time consuming, but I stuck with it, determined not to give up. I was promoted and moved to another department.

Throughout that time, I was the light of the office. My attitude and hard work had an affect on my co-workers; I was the youngest employee, it was like being the life of the party. People admired my fresh ideas and methods of handling my work.

Nearly 18 months into my new found career, I was totally displeased with my job. The change in department brought on a different workload that did not pair well with my abilities or personality. I was working harder and falling further and further behind. I had no motivation or desire to get out of bed in the morning because I dreaded going to work. I came to the realization that this career was not for me.

The discontentment of the job reflected in my work and in other areas of my life. I was unhappy a lot. I could not figure it out; I thought my measure of success was wrapped in having a lucrative job and working my way to the top of my career. I was told by many people, "if you can just get an education, work hard at a career, success is bound to follow". So here I was working harder everyday, doing something that I did not like for the sake of success.

I prayed constantly about my situation, asked others to pray, but there was no movement from this job. There was no outlet. I held on to the promise of Jeremiah 29:11 and trusted God to work the situation out on my behalf.

After three and half years, I was released from that job. The separation was mutual and I had become so emotionally tired and physically fed up that the release of the thing was a burden lifted from my shoulders. This Release caused joy to overflow in me. I didn't know where it came from, but finally, I felt as though I could do what God was calling me to do without restraint.

I felt a peace that passed all of my understanding. I was going into a place of uncertainty because I did not know where my career was headed, when the next job opportunity would come or where this would lead. However God's peace remained. There was faith and what I felt did not waver, so I knew what I had encountered was not of my own doing. In the midst of a downward economy and scarce job security, I had a sense of wholeness I could not explain. I felt F.R.E.E and knew that I was not losing. I was gaining something much more than I could contemplate at the time.

In my situation, the Release was not orchestrated until 3 and half years of work. It took me that long to gain all of the lessons that the situation was designed to teach me. God was teaching me endurance, patience, contentment and strength in the midst of a seemingly negative situation. The most valuable lesson was contentment; I had to learn to trust him even though I did not like the situation that I was in. God was teaching me to stand in spite of what I was facing. This same lesson of contentment has taught me to look for the meaning in things because I know that there is a reason that I am going through the things that I face.

If you find yourself in a place of discontentment and you are searching for an answer to it, start with asking God. Ask him to open your eyes to the steps that you need to take to find a place of comfort and contentment for your life. If it can happen for me, it can happen for you as well.

This type of comfort and contentment only happens when you decide to hold on to the promises of God. Everything that is happening is intended for an expected end and you must stand firm on this and by faith act on it.

If God made you a promise, you can stand and believe that what is happening with you is contributing to what He has promised you.

If God made you a promise, you can stand and believe that what is happening with you is contributing to what He has promised you. God's word has to be fulfilled and he is using you my friend to accomplish it. Whether that means standing still or moving forward, follow the direction that God is giving and you are sure to make the right decision.

A very important aspect of a Release is that it will not happen until the life lessons are extracted. The lesson has to fulfill what it is designated to teach. I believe a lot of valuable time in our lives is wasted when we continue to go through the same situations again and again because we are not learning the intended lessons. In this case, repetition does not spell perfection. Learn the lesson and move on to the next place you need to go.

Once I was released from the job and unemployment set in, I had to change my perception about being in that state. I never wanted to be unemployed in fact it was one of my biggest fears. However, I had to be unemployed in order to learn the lessons that were attached to it. I learned to be content with the fact that I was not working and I learned to do all things to the glory of God.
As my perception changed, God began to minister to me about his work and his plans for me. During those months of unemployment, God gave me insight on my life purpose which was something that I was continuously seeking. Standing on the promises of God's word during that time was a source of help and strength that I could not obtain on my own, it was priceless.

When I learned the lessons of Release, I transitioned. My next job was an answer to my prayers. I was Released with an opportunity to experience the next level of the journey.

The Timing of a Thing

Timing is imperative during a period of Release. It is absolutely essential to move at the right moment for the right reason. When we allow God to orchestrate our steps, timing is not in our complete control. However we are still responsible to move when directed. As we move, we receive instructions every step of the way.

In his infinite wisdom God has calculated the moments of our lives. When we move in God's timing, a Release is timely and paired perfectly with the situation. Looking back at my first career experience, if I would have thrown up my hands and quit my job, God would not have been able to provide a large separation incentive for me. I would have been so caught up in looking for provision that I would have missed the lessons that God had for me during unemployment.

There is provision in timing.

There is provision in timing. When God has ordained you to do a thing and move in the light of releasing something or someone, he always makes a way. It is his character as our Father to provide. In our obedience, we find exactly what we need. He loves us so dearly and requires our obedience especially during a time when he wants F.R.E.Edom to be a part of our lives.

Seasons are not only for nature, the same cycle of growth and change apply to our lives. In Ecclesiastes 3:1 Solomon (one of the world's wisest men) wrote, "There is a time for everything, and a season for every activity under heaven. " (NIV) In verses 2-8, he proceeds to give examples of times that have come and gone, all of which we can identify with personally and collectively. When we understand that growth and change are part of the pattern of the world, we better understand and accept that our life situation is subject to be different at any time.

God allows us to experience seasons of life where things and people are added to us and sometimes taken away from us as well. When it is time for a release, rest assured God had it on his mind since the beginning of time. He knows what is happening to us, and he cares. We must trust his timing and his desire to release from us and to us. By doing this we allow him to perform his perfect work in us.

Loneliness vs. Being Alone

There is a difference between being lonely and being alone. Loneliness is a perception that can occur at any time even in the presence of other people. The fact that the space around a person is occupied does not determine how he or she feels inside. Loneliness can be accompanied by feelings of abandonment, rejection and a host of other feelings that can lead to depressed thoughts and actions.

Loneliness is a state of mind, more so than a physical state. You could be by yourself and never feel alone. The fact that no one is around you does not make you feel lonely. In some cases (especially when you are a parent) alone time is a luxury! Rest assured loneliness and being alone are two very different things.

Being alone allows time to rejuvenate. For busy individuals, I encourage you to spend time alone just to become one with yourself. Some of the greatest revelations have come when I was spending time alone. This sort of time is most definitely valuable when you are seeking direction and instruction from God about your life. I think of being alone as a place of solitude, which is free of outside distraction and interruption.

There is always a purpose in alone time. This place of solitude is not designed to make you feel bad. It is for your growth and the development of your purpose. When I released from my job, my days became very different, most of my time was spent alone, gathering my thoughts and honestly writing this book. Without the time to regroup, listen and gather strength from God's presence during that time, the events of life could have become very, very strenuous.

Have you ever tried to hold a conversation with someone at a football game? The crowd is cheering, people are dancing, and it is a really tough thing to hold a conversation in the midst of a crowd. The person can not hear you and as a result they are most likely not comprehending the message you are trying to get to them. It is the same way with communicating with God.

If he is trying to get a message to you, but there is so much going on around you that you can not comprehend, it is certain that something said will be missed. The lesson of listening may very well be the answer to the alone factor that one is experiencing.

Alone time brings you face to face with the reality of yourself.

Alone time brings you face to face with the reality of yourself. Some of us look in the mirror and we don't like what we see. An observation period is needed to fully assess these dislikes. When we spend time alone, it allows time for self reflection.

Make a list of things that you like and do not like about yourself. Pray and ask God to reveal to you ways that you can change some of the dislikes that you have. He will speak, be careful and intentional when following his instructions. Ask God to reveal what he is trying to help you see or understand.

Whatever your goals are for change; set a plan in motion to accomplish them. When you have a moment, go over them in your mind and imagine yourself accomplishing your goal and the outcome of those accomplishments. Growth and change will inevitably take place when you take time to self reflect. It will cause you to change your perception of loneliness and the Release that you have experienced.

The turning point of alone time brings elevation into your life. Elevation is the reason that you may have been released and are currently going through a period of alone time. Going to the next level is the arrival at a place that is not familiar to you. You will need time to acclimate yourself to your new level of growth. Give yourself solitary time to do this.

The elevation that God would like you to experience is not for everyone and in order to instruct you in the correct path while you journey, walking alone at this point is inevitable.

People have a tendency of giving their opinions; it can be solicited and other times it is not. Their viewpoints are not God's viewpoints. His ways are not our ways, nor his thoughts, our thoughts. This does not mean that the assistance of others is not needed, however God will orchestrate and instruct an intervention when it is necessary. Be very careful about who you speak with, share with and commune with during an alone period in life, your elevation and progress may depend on it.

The Importance of Connection

In most instances relationships bring joy into our lives. They give us companionship, someone to commune with and a sense of importance and belonging.

Release especially in the case of a relationship (whether that is a professional or personal one) is a time of separation and unwarranted solitude. This is a heavy feeling because there may not be an outlet for expression; however this is just a perception.

"I will never leave you nor forsake" Joshua 1:5 (NIV) is a promise we can hold on to when loneliness is present. God will never leave you or forsake you. His desire is not for you to feel lonely, but to ask for his comforting presence to meet you right where you are. The whole point of the lonely feeling may be to ask for God's comforting presence.

Loneliness has its lessons. When perceived correctly it can be a valuable time in life. It is in these times of quietness that God reveals the most to you. If you listen long enough to hear the freedom in God's voice inviting you to commune with him. If you do not know the voice of God, begin with prayer. Through prayer, you communicate with God. Since communication is a two way street, God will communicate with you. There may not be a cracking of the sky or a sign (like Moses' burning bush) for you to see, but God will speak with you in a way that you will understand. He made you and knows you best. God communicates with each of us individually and in a different ways. When he speaks, you will know in your heart that it is his voice.

Communication with God is essential.

Communication with God is essential. In order for growth to take place in a relationship there must be a line of open communication. God does not desire to be your butler, magician or genie; he desires to be the rock of your salvation, the vine that connects you to his provision.

In John 15:4 Jesus likens our relationship with Him as a vine and a branch of the vine. "Remain in me and I will remain in you." (NIV)

The branch is an extension of the vine that is continually connected. The vine provides strength for the branch's growth. Without the vine, the branch can not produce anything. He was not asking the branches to go and try to produce fruit on their own, he only asks us to remain in him. In his presence is the fullness of communion where there is no loneliness, only the opportunity for him to be our strong vine in which we can grow and thrive. How can we ever truly be alone when we are connected in this way?

Ways to Hear God's Voice

In the process of communicating with God we have to be able to recognize when he is speaking to us.

God speaks very clearly through his word: the Bible. The bible is God's instruction manual to humanity. It is a compass through the journey of this world; it is our assurance, and his promises are listed time and time again. Becoming a student of God's Word is a powerful asset. We draw strength for our journey through His Word. We come to realize that God's word is forever settled.

Today, there are many versions of the Bible, from the King James translation, which is hundreds of years old, to a New American standard, which is literal in its transition of words and meanings. If the wording in one translation is difficult to understand, choose one that is right for you. It helps greatly to read and understand the Word of God so you can determine what he is saying to you very clearly.

God also speaks through the assembly of his people-the Church. God speaks in many ways in church. It maybe a song the choir is singing, a prayer that is prayed, or a verse of scripture that speaks to your heart. You may hear God speak through the sermon that is being shared by a pastor. These are various ways of hearing God's voice at church. The key is to be sensitive enough to know when God is speaking. The primary goal of hearing God's voice at church is to prompt people to have a personal relationship with Him. Assembling together with believers is a great way to start to recognize God's voice and the beginning of your communication with him.

The third way to hear God speak is through a personal relationship with Him. This is where the majority of instruction, direction, counsel, and communion will take place. Remember how it feels when someone you know well calls your name? You do not have to second guess whose voice it is; you know who it was because you have a relationship with that person. This aspect is no different with God; the more time you spend communing with him, the more you grow familiar with his voice. God speaks to us based on your relationship with Him. The main way that he uses is through the Holy Spirit, which is the third part of the Trinity. The spirit ministers in a still, small assuring voice.

As Release is taking place, it is very important to recognize God's voice in the midst of what is going on. This is the way to cope with the ever-changing people and situations of the Release process. God is a constant, grounded source of strength when everything else seems unstable. Listening for guidance, instruction, and comfort allow Release to contribute to F.R.E.Edom even in the darkest hour of your life.

God is doing a great work in your life. Embrace the solitary walk, the time is necessary for your F.R.E.Edom to be complete. In time your mind will be renewed and rejuvenated. You will find strength to continue on your journey. If God has spoken to you about being elevated and progressing rest assured that he has equipped you to handle the solitary portion of the journey.

5

Released

From the Pit to the Palace

The State of Bondage

We can not talk about Release without observing its opposite–bondage. Bondage is a subject that many prefer not to think about and as a result refuse to admit when it is actually present. Bondage is a state of being under unwanted security. It is restricting. It is binding. Bondage can exists internally and externally—it is not defined by a place. It is a state of mind that must be broken in order for F.R.E.Edom to exist.

I have never been incarcerated, but I have gained a clear understanding from people who have experienced it. Incarceration is a state of restraint and continual monitoring. Someone tells you what to do: where to go, when to eat, sleep and work. There is virtually not one moment of the prison life that is not calculated or scheduled by someone else. The mindset of most incarcerated individuals is one that permeates with the mentality of being guarded in their actions and provided for by the institution.

Once a prisoner returns to society, the new found freedom of life beyond the prison walls is an unfamiliar scene. The mentality of prison life continues to manifest itself. The person may not know what to do, where to go or even how to conduct his or herself without the direction of someone else.

As a result the same behavioral pattern that led to trouble can resurface landing him or her in the former state of imprisonment. This is the behavior of a "repeat offender". Often repeat offenders will express their desire to be free, but there are no changes in the behavioral pattern to accommodate this desire. As a result, the offender returns to what is familiar and seemingly right in their eyes.

Statistics show that 56 percent of violent felons had prior convictions. In some U.S states, statistics show that 75 percent of individuals convicted have a prior record. Why are these statistics so staggering? Repeat offenders are people who have allowed their bondage to infiltrate every area of their lives. The physical state of bondage has dictated to them how they will act and conduct themselves whether they are inside or outside of an institution. This bondage is mental and becomes one of the major hindrances in the lives of former prisoners.

Does this cycle seem familiar? Some of us who have never experienced incarceration are serving life as "repeat offenders". Living in a state of mental, spiritual or emotional bondage is not healthy or productive. These negative factors are given permission to determine what we believe about ourselves and how we will conduct our lives. Life remains unchanged and the vicious cycle of our behavior continues to render the same results. The problems maybe recognizable, but if there is no change of routine or habits, how can there be released from living as a repeat offender? The answer is the Great Exchange.

The Great Exchange

We are F.R.E.E to live a life that rests in God and liberated from habits and routines of the past. God lights our pathway allowing us to have sight in a dark world. Psalms 146:7b-8 says, "The Lord sets prisoners free, the Lord gives sight to the blind, the Lord lifts us up those who are bowed down, and the Lord loves the righteous" (NIV)

The answer to breaking the cycle of the repeat offender mentality lies in the desire to live differently from the life of the past.

We are free to live a liberated life.

We are free to live a liberated life. It is making a conscious effort to believe what God believes about you. In order to live free walls must be destroyed. The prison of fear, doubt, rebellion and unrest and many other negative factors play a role in constructing walls of bondage. These four walls (and others for that matter) construct a prison that is built primarily by the person sitting in the cell. When walls are constructed, they serve a dual purpose. Walls do not allow anything to come in and nothing goes out, there is no exchange.

Being completely honest with God and yourself will cause walls to come down in your life. Identifying things that are sources of bondage for you will greatly help as well. It does not require perfection, just a will to admit it and ask for help. At the first sign of habits, memories or people that represent bondage do your best to remove it. Pray and ask God to replace it with thoughts and acts of liberation. Practice putting these feelings behind you and constantly dwell on things that will serve as a source of Release. When there is a desire for change and your actions begin to reflect this, God is willing to be a guide every step of the way.

When we decide to be F.R.E.E, the walls begin to come down through the power of God. As the walls are destroyed, God gives life in exchange for death, assurance in exchange for fear, and peace in exchange for unrest. My friend this is the Great Exchange. We are then in a position to give and receive from those around us. A life that is free of walls is characterized by flowing F.R.E.Edom and Release has taken place. What a wonderful feeling right? The exchange is available to you right now just believe and surrender today so that you may experience the release that is leading you to F.R.E.Edom.

The Changed Prisoner

As defined by some, the purpose of prison is rehabilitation. People serve time because they have offended society or broken the law. For all prisoners, incarceration is a life altering experience, but for some it is a life changing one as well.

For these individuals while they are in bondage, the chains began to speak and a conscious decision is made that their lives will not be confined by the stigma of a prisoner. An elevation of thinking takes place that allows them to be free. This liberation exists even though bondage surrounds them. Their minds transcend to a place that has no barriers, guard ship and the feeling of liberation is alive and well in their hearts.

Change is evident in this prisoner because the mind and heart made a decision to behave differently thus affecting the physical behavior. Incarceration is only a physical state for this type of prisoner because liberation resides on the inside. Life is not viewed through the length of a sentence. The mental release has already occurred and the physical state of release will eventually catch up.

There are dozens of stories about individuals who made decisions while they were in physical bondage to take hold of their lives and live reformed and restored. In the maximum security sector of Leeukop, a prison located in Northern Johannesburg, South Africa there is a man serving time. He was found guilty of 2 counts of murder and 3 counts of attempted murder during a period of political crimes in the country and is currently serving a prison sentence. He admitted to the crimes he is accused of, but desired to turn his life into a positive experience for the sake of his wife and five children. He says that he was inspired to turn around by a sign that read: "I was born to succeed and not to fail. I was born to triumph against defeat."

For this man, the road to rehabilitation began in 2001 out of a desire to be a good example for his children and the youth of South Africa. He became involved in a program called From Pillar to Post, which is designed to detour school age children against committing crimes that will land them in prison. He is now a living example of mental liberation and serves his community by urging others to learn from his mishappenings. He is living life as a new creation and discovering purpose by helping others.

When we submit our lives to Christ we have the opportunity to embrace this newness. 2 Corinthians 5:17 emphasizes "Therefore if any man be in Christ, he is a new creature: old things are passed away; behold, all things become new." (KJV) We are new creatures and if we are, this means that the physical state of our surroundings does not define who we are. Prisoners that have received a newness of life have found hope in this. Even though they are not physically free or they are enjoying a newness that characterizes who they are from the inside out.

Prison can not restrain a F.R.E.E person. Prison can't kill a spirit no matter if it is a physical one or one constructed in the mind. Release is internal before it is external. Countless prisoners have found liberation and the ability to rise from their spiritual prisons from the inside out. The life of the prisoner is changed and the effects that follow are endless.

Miraculously F.R.E.E

We see an example of the unstoppable prisoner in the story of Paul and Silas. Paul and Silas were taken to prison for proclaiming the name of Christ in a place that did not believe in God. However, their physical state as prisoners was not a definition of who they were. Their minds were so elevated and free that it allowed them to praise and worship God in their bondage.

Acts 16:23-26:

After they had been severely flogged (beaten), they were thrown into prison, and the jailer was commanded to guard them carefully. Upon receiving such orders, he put them in the inner cell and fastened their feet in the stocks. About midnight Paul and Silas were praying and singing hymns to God, and the other prisoners were listening to them. Suddenly there was such a violent earthquake that the foundations of the prison were shaken. At once all the prison doors flew open, and everybody's chains came loose. (NIV)

Paul and Silas' praise changed the atmosphere of their situation. God was able to work on their behalf when they chose to praise in the midst of what they were experiencing.

While they praised others heard them. This act of admiration proved to others that they were witnesses of a mighty God. Even though praising God in a prison may have seemed unorthodox, this act set the groundwork for a miracle.

The factor of faith caused God to demonstrate a supernatural experience on behalf of the prisoners. Faith is what we hope for and the evidence of what we can not see. God rewards us based on our faith. God delivered Paul and Silas when he saw the level of their faithfulness. They were falsely accused and their imprisoned state was not the best. Through this prison experience, God increased the faith of Paul and Silas. He tested them to see if they would honor him even in a state of imprisonment and wrongful punishment. It moved the heart of God to see Paul and Silas worshipping in their current state. Not only did God move on their behalf and set them free from bondage, he allowed the other prisoners to experience liberation as well. When the earthquake occurred, it loosed the bands of all the prisoners. Faith freed everyone.

God does the same for his children today. He orchestrates circumstances to build and test faith.

God's desire is not to see you breakdown, it is to see you breakthrough.

God's desire is not to see you breakdown, it is to see you breakthrough. He proves his faithfulness while you establish and place trust in him. As you walk the journey set before you, you become a witness to God's faithfulness. Other people are placed around you to observe your experiences as well. You will come out with a testimony of great faith that benefits others and allows you to experience God deeper.

A decision to be released is a dedicated decision. It is one that denies inconsistency, double-mindedness and doubt. When you encounter confusion it must be counteracted with faith. Faith spearheads our journey into F.R.E.Edom and it allows clear insight into God's plan. The question must be answered: Will I trust God through faith? Or rely on past decisions to make a choice about the future.

Release: On the Brink of Breakthrough

In the Bible, we find one of the greatest examples of transition ever told in the story of Joseph (Genesis 37-50). This was truly a Pit-to-Palace story with many stops along the way. Joseph was a young dreamer who could interpret dreams and he was his father's favored son. He was forced to leave his home by his brothers out of their hatred, who left him in a pit and sold him into slavery. His departure (Release) from his Father's house was not a choice of his own. It was the first of Joseph's unfavorable situations.

Joseph transitioned many times. He was enslaved, released from Potipher's house, and thrown in jail for two years. While in jail, he did not lose hope. He held on to his faith that deliverance was coming. In the end Joseph's gift of interpreting dreams lead him to be elevated as overseer of Pharaoh's kingdom. His gift made room for him and he used it for the glory of God.

The transitions throughout Joseph's life held purpose. The reason all of this was happening to Joseph was not for his detriment; it was for him to realize that God was to be glorified. He was RELEASED from a pit to a prison and then exalted to be something that was bigger than himself.

Joseph was an example of God's release, process and progression. The beauty of Joseph's releases lie the notion that Joseph had no power within himself to change his bondage situations. God did not ask Joseph to walk in the light of his own wisdom and release himself. God wanted Joseph to fully rely on him. In turn, he provided favor, blessings and provision for Joseph during his entire journey. Joseph gained wisdom through each Release moment he encountered.

God never allowed him to be released and alone without provision. Even when it took some time, he orchestrated and purposefully led Joseph's steps along the path. Nothing ever comes quickly or haphazardly; it is a part of a divine plan that is masterfully and uniquely pieced together by the Creator.

Handling Uncertainty

Moving forward after a Release is not an option, it is a necessity.

Moving forward after a Release is not an option, it is a necessity. Progression can bring uncertainty. When there is a Release of something, a job, a relationship or other possessions there is an uncertainty that follows the loss. The uncertainty arises because there is a change or a breaking of a habit or routine. What is normal is now not happening regularly and it is causing uncertainty to lure in the mind and heart. With this uncertainty comes fear, this emotion can be paralyzing.

If this sounds familiar to you, believe me, you are not alone. This is a feeling that is common in transition and when a Release is happening there is evidence of a transition. As life takes place, changes and continues to simply happen, transition will occur and uncertainty during that time is more than likely. The key is not if, but when will it occur. How transition is handled is a good indicator of how the Release is being handled. If the transition is not going well, the Release is not being seen from a beneficial standpoint.

The key to overcoming uncertainty is to continue to walk. It is important that we understand that Release and transition are a part of growth even if it doesn't appear as such at first. The fear of what you can not see may tempt you to stop, I encourage you to keep walking. Liberation and Release always outweigh the bondage of the familiar.

It is important that we understand that in our Release lies our F.R.E.Edom. Release is a part of the process. Everything has its time and season; we must accept release when it is happening. When release is taking place it is important to accept it and not hold on out of a need or a want. God knows what is best for us and as a result we must follow his lead in all that concerns our live.

Release is not an easy place to be and it does require one to relinquish control of the circumstances of life and this is not a simple task for most. It can be accomplished, even though uncertainty may hang in the balance. God knows the ending from the beginning. If he knows how your journey will end before you even begin the journey, who better to trust with the details?

When uncertainty arises and it most definitely will, it is important to pray about your process and journey. Human nature causes us to become creatures of habit. We gravitate to activities that make us most comfortable. We must allow God to be our blessed assurance in the face of uncertainty. As we pray, he releases us to experience his spirit, as we desire his presence, he reveals himself to us. Jeremiah 29:13 says, "You will seek me and find me when you seek me will all your heart." (NIV) We must seek what he is trying to say to us and understand that he is not the author of confusion. What we are encountering when it comes to uncertainty is the fact that we can not see exactly where we are headed, but the one that is leading us most certainly does. We are designed to follow the path that is set before us by God and when we do this, leaving our uncertainty behind, we can walk with confidence into our tomorrow.

When faced with uncertainty remember that there is a bright future you are destined to embrace.

When faced with uncertainty remember that there is a bright future you are destined to embrace. The wilderness of the uncertainty that you are facing is leading you to the F.R.E.E life. Hold on to the promises of God's word and stand on what he has told you about your future. Refuse to allow your circumstances to dictate what is occurring around you because there is always more than one thing taking place. What you can not see is benefiting you more than what is seen. If you remember these keys of power, they will ignite your engine to destiny. Continue to walk and embrace all that is in front of you, even when your sight says otherwise.

God Wants You to Be the Example

God desires for you to be an example of Release to this world. The next time a moment of Release happens in your life, look at it through the lenses of the future. The Bible says, what we see is temporal, but what we do not see is eternal. Release is not always what it looks like. There is something greater that God desires for us to see and ultimately become. The perception of the Release has to be correctly positioned with purpose in order to fully experience what God is saying and doing in us. For this reason God wants you to be the example of the Release to greater place in Him.

Remember Release is a part of the journey, but Release is not where the story ends. There is a new chapter and you are destined to make it there. The Release can be accompanied by many emotions ranging from liberation to loneliness, but do not get caught on that coat hook— finish the course. Even when there are moments of solitude, there is still purpose in what you are walking through and seeking the lesson is where the greatest victory is found. When we take time to listen to God and understand the purpose of our Release, we benefit greatly from it and have the opportunity to journey toward the destiny that he is leading us to.

None of this is for your detriment, only for your advancement and around each corner greatness is calling and waiting for you to answer. Walk through this time and know that there is more of the journey God desires for you to experience.

6

Experience
Life's Puzzle Pieces

Life's Stepping Stones

The Marriage that ended in divorce, the death of a loved one, the cancer that is spreading, an alcoholic parent, the troubles of the past…..Linked? Can something good come from this? Why… How?

The contributing factors of Finally and Release moments comprise the experiences of life. These experiences are linked together to lead to a place of mental, spiritual and emotional awakening. Experience is a central theme in reaching F.R.E.Edom because it is absolutely vital to our existence as humanity.

There can not be F.R.E.Edom on your journey without the vital link of Experience.

There can not be F.R.E.Edom on your journey without the vital link of Experience. Being that experiences are vital to our humanity, it is important that we learn to utilize them for growth, development and identifying purpose.

Life experiences shape, teach, mold, and instill many different perspectives. As we live, experiences bring altering thoughts and opinions that are leading to the reception of life's lessons. Experiences lead to places that we said we may never go, while other experiences lead us to places that we could have only imagined.

As we look at the fabric of our lives and what we have become, we draw from our past experiences and see where, why and how these moments have affected us. Whether the experiences were from childhood or adulthood, they left relevant impressions that are not easily erased. Experience holds the key to reasoning, they help to explain why we do what we do and why we believe what we believe.

Life's Puzzle

How did you get to this very moment in life? What has shaped you along the way? If you have ever asked yourself these questions, they require reflection. As you mature and reflect on experiences, your eyes will be opened to the lessons that serve as stepping stones to growth and elevated thinking. Experience plays a paramount role in asking ourselves these vital questions and can hold the light to our answers as well. Reflecting on the past brings about an opportunity to see the lessons that God designed with clarity.

I like to think of experiences as pieces of a puzzle. Puzzles are comprised of small pieces that function together to form a larger picture. Puzzles are complex and detailed, but once complete the full picture can be seen. This is done by viewing life as fragmented pieces that fit perfectly together to form a picture that becomes the masterpiece of its creator.

When we view experiences as essential pieces of our lives that are designed to fit perfectly together, we will begin to see the beauty in all experiences. Whether these moments foster happiness, sadness, pain, joy, anger or resentment, one thing holds true of them; they are distinctive, contributing parts of life's puzzle. The master of all creation has designed each piece. As we learn to look beyond the circumstances and exterior of the experience, it is discovered how all of the small parts are working together for the advancement of our lives and purpose.

Romans 8:28 sums this up very well: "And we know that all things work together for good to them that love God, to them who are the called according to his purpose." This verse holds the key to life's experiences and tells us what God's purpose was for giving us the experiences.

The passage did not say all things happy, joyful and wonderful work together for our good, it said ALL things work together for our good. God desires to free us to live according to his purpose. He wants us to experience the goodness of who he is through every single thing that we walk through. He has designed our lives in such a way that our experiences become stepping stones to finding great purpose on earth. What we are called to do and what we are meant to become is wrapped up in learning how to purposefully walk through every experience of our lives and expand to a place that brings to light the freedom we are called to.

When you set out on a journey, you expect it to lead somewhere. No one aimlessly walks on a journey. It is planned, carefully mapped out and designed to bring one to an expected end. The journey along this road of life is set up the same way, in Jeremiah 29:11 "For I know the plans I have for you,", declares the Lord, "plans to prosper you and not to harm you, plans to give you hope and a future." God desires your journey to be one that causes you prosper. Prospering means to function in wholeness, nothing is missing or broken when true prosperity is present. Monetary prosperity only scratches the surface when it comes to how God wants us to prosper. He wants you to be whole from the inside out; bringing you to the expected end that will not only cause you to be fully prosperous, but will bring glory and honor to his name.

What you experience on this road of life is extremely valuable to where you are going.

What you experience on this road of life is extremely valuable to where you are going. Jeremiah 29:11 emphasizes that there are plans designed to give you hope and a future. Your life and future are purposefully designed and fulfilling the assignment in a way by which you glorify Him. God did not design what you experienced to permanently damage you; it was made to cause you to find hope in him.

How to Utilize Experience

What can be learned from the past? What is the purpose of the present? I have asked myself these questions many times. God has brought me to a point in my life that I truly believe that experiences are always tailored to teach something. The past, the virtue of the present and the promise of the future are hinged on the ability to recognize how your experiences are linked together to lead to expansion.

It becomes a matter of asking God, "what is the purpose of this?" instead of "why am I experiencing this?" When the focus becomes the "what" and not the "why", a deeper meaning is discovered. The purpose of the experience may not lie on the surface of the situation. It may take some searching, but the important thing is to realize that purpose does exist.

There are four deeper meanings that answer the question of what. Pinpointing the deeper meaning behind an experience will allow you to utilize the experience as an opportunity to grow.

The first reason for an experience is to point out a strength or weakness. We do not know what we have inside until it is tested. Tests teach us a lot about ourselves because we get a chance to see how we will react or handle a situation. Experiences are tests of great strength and the identifiers of great weakness. God promises in his word to be our strength in the time of trouble. When we see that our situation is pointing out a weakness in our lives, it is important to rely on God to strengthen us through whatever we face. I have found great comfort in God's strength through experiences of weakness in my life. The point of weakness that we possess becomes the point of grace and strength when we learn to rely on God.

The second is to cause a defining moment. In this moment which we decide to be conquerors over our situations or conquered by them. This deeper meaning deals with the factor of overcoming adversity. It poises the question, "what will I fight for" and "what will I allow to defeat me" it points out determination and endurance. Many of life's lessons are learned through the pathways of pain, suffering, and hurt. This is how we know we can fight and most importantly that we can overcome. For some people it is a physical illness, an addiction, a relationship problem, or even internal battles with the one looking in the mirror. This deeper meaning leaves the conqueror changed and positioned to help others overcome as well.

Third, experiences take place to give you a testimony. There is no testimony without a test. Whether it is the testing of faith, love, devotion, or anything else our lives are shaken to see how anchored we really are. After I wrote this book the viewpoints that I share and the reasoning behind writing the book were tested. During that time I read my own book to find the encouragement to press on. Today my testimony and message of F.R.E.Edom is greater because of the tests I experienced.

Lastly, experiences serve as a way to discover the characteristics of God. Some experiences we face are simply out of our control. It is in these moments that God wants to display aspects of who he is to us. When a need arises, he is Jehovah Jireh, "Our Provider", when trouble is present he is Jehovah Nissi "Our great peace" and in every situation he is the great "I am". Our relationship with God is cultivated through experiences we face, it is when we learn to look to him that we experience the magnitude of who he is.

A young pastor was abandoned by both of his parents at birth and was taken in by his aunt. His aunt raised him in the knowledge of Christ and he became a Christian at a young age. When his aunt passed away during his teenage years, he knew no other family members. He was forced to live on the streets as a homeless teenager with no shelter or provision. As a result he began to sleep under a bridge and did this for several years. While under that bridge, this young man came to know Christ in a very real and personal way, he later went on to become a phenomenal pastor and teacher. God used him to pastor two churches that experienced extraordinary growth under his leadership. Under his leadership, many people were taught God's word and became followers of Christ.

Later in the pastor's life he met his biological father for the first time. He discovered that his father was an abusive alcoholic and most of his siblings were addicted to alcohol as well. God used this pastor's homeless experience to build a lasting relationship with him. The pastor's life could have been drastically different if he would have been in the care of his biological father and under the influence of his siblings.

In this story all four of the deeper meanings can be seen. This young man's weakness and lack of provision was evident through his homeless experience. He overcame his tragic situations and came out of it with an undeniable testimony. Through it all, the young man came to know God in an extraordinary way. We don't always understand what God is doing and why he allows things to happen the way they do, but experiences are all a part of the divine plan that he has for each of us.

Take a moment and reflect on one of your experiences. What thoughts come to mind? Are the memories exciting, fearful, happy, intimidating, or worrisome? What was the outcome? Whatever you remember most about the experience is where you can start looking for the deeper meaning behind it. Once you see the lesson in the experience, ask yourself how is this contributing to the person that I am? This is where growth takes place and the experience produces great benefit for you and those around you.

The Victim's Mentality

Why did this happen to me?, I can't because of......, My life would be so much better off if it wasn't for.....Have you ever heard or used any of these phrases? These statements are made from the thought process called the victim's mentality. When this mental hold is present, it is constantly causing every action or the lack thereof to be held against the canvas of a painful past. This includes current behavior traits, habits and the thought process as well. There is always a need to relive the victim's point of reference and make it relevant to the present.

When people are at a place of hurt and they can not deal with it within themselves, it will be released onto others. The victim's mentality takes part by allowing the offender to believe that their damaging action is justified because of a hurtful experience in their past. The offender's mentality is: *someone* did this to me, so I will do this to someone else. This creates a continued cycle of hurt for the offender.

We all have experiences that we allowed to victimize us; knowingly or unknowingly some of our actions are a result of our hurtful experiences of the past.

When we allow ourselves to become victims of our past, we do not walk boldly into the future.

When we allow ourselves to become victims of our past, we do not walk boldly into the future. The "victim's mentality" is one that paints a simultaneous picture of guilt and blame. The part of this mentality is that it stops a person from moving forward.

God has freed us to live as conquerors. We are called to conquer. We are given the power to overcome every experience of the past, deriving from it the positive lesson that leads to our expansion. In Romans Paul wrote, "No, in all these things we are more than conquerors through Him who loved us." (Rom. 8:37 NIV) Paul was referring to the persecution of Christians which included danger, hardship, trouble, famine and even death. He was inspired by God to write that verse of faith in the midst of all of those horrible experiences. God has given us the same faith to be free and conquer. He gives us the opportunity to have victory over everything that stands in our way of F.R.E.Edom.

In order to live the F.R.E.E life, we must believe through faith that it is possible. Through prayer we can confess *"God, this happened, but I do not want to live as a victim to it because that is not your design. Help me to see the lesson that you have called me to learn and leave the mentality of bondage behind."*

When we begin to take steps away from the victim's mentality and combine it with faith, we step into expansion. The first three letters of victim are VIC, these are also the first three letters of VICTORY. How the word ends is up to you, choose wisely and let your choice line up with God's design for your life.

Handling Issues once and for all

As we live and experience the many situations of life, we encounter moments that cause negative emotions within us. These memories have a way of reminding us of a painful place that we would rather not remember; it maybe an abusive situation from childhood or neglect at the hand of an adult, molestation or abandonment, verbal abuse that created mental scars or a tragic event. All of these experiences can be seen as life altering, leaving us with feelings and memories that are not easily erased.

People cope with these types of situations in many different ways. Some choose not to deal with them at all. When we choose not to properly handle the negative experiences of our past, we will constantly view present and future situations against the backdrop of the negative experience. The only way to stop this vicious cycle is to handle the issues. Not just on the surface, but really get to the bottom of the negative experiences so they can be handled in a way that brings healing.

Handling deep issues is never easy. It will cause an array of emotions to arise, but there is a way to get started that can lead to good results. The first step is to confront it, you can not change what you are not willing to recognize. Recognizing that there is a problem and that there is a root to the problem is the first step to addressing the problem.

Second, ask for help and seek advice, pray first about who you should speak to concerning your issues. It is important to have the right support system, who ever God leads you to speak with will play a great role in assisting you.

Third, relinquish fear. Fear is debilitating which slows or stops the progress of healing. Get over the fear by looking at the reality of the situation and renouncing thoughts that do not promote progress.

Last, decide to live for the better. This is a mental choice that can only be made by you. No one can decide how you will live your life. You have to make a conscious choice to live in a way that is conducive to your continued growth and development. Making this decision will determine other important decisions in your life. You can live better knowing that you first made a choice to do so. The battle is mental and spiritual before it is ever physical, make the decision and you will be on a great road to dealing with difficult issues.

Live New, Live F.R.E.E

In this chapter we have spoken about experiences, overcoming adversity and ultimately finding growth through the experiences of the past.

Your past experiences do not determine the beauty of your future.

Your past experiences do not determine the beauty of your future. When you let go of the victim's mentality and allow God to take the pain and produce purpose, you begin to conquer. Your life can become new in the midst of all you have experienced. 2 Corinthians 5:17 says: "Therefore if any man be in Christ, he is a new creature: old things have passed away; behold, all things are become new." (NIV) That includes you!

When you encounter God you encounter change. Spiritual hinderance does not have to be a part of your life, God has liberated you. Living new is a continual growth into the destiny that God has called you to do and become. New life allows you to maximize the present by fulfilling purpose and effectively impact the future.

You are no longer a slave to your past or the things of it. John 8:36-37 is a great expression of this, it says, "Now a slave has no permanent place in the family, but a son belongs to it forever. So if the Son sets you free, you will be free indeed." (NIV) Living as a son (or daughter) of the most high provides liberation and you have an open invitation to enjoy it.

7

Experience
The Lesson Within

Trust and Experiencing God

Trust is a driving force in relationships and we have a natural tendency to only trust those that we know. In order to truly cultivate a relationship, the element of trust has to be there. It is essential to the growth of any relationship. Where there is no trust, it is very difficult to act with confidence. The same element of trust is required when we come to know God. God allows the experiences we face to teach us how to trust him more.

There is not a moment in our existence that is not a part of his plan. Even when his hand does not seem present, we must remember that God leaves nothing to chance and he tailors the lesson of our lives to increase our faith. To see these lessons and possess greater purpose we must trust him. "For my thoughts are not your thoughts, neither are your ways my ways. (Isaiah 55:8 NIV) " This simply means that until we experience God and take on his mindset, we cannot see things from his perspective. Experiencing God is experiencing faith.

Trusting God's Answers

Have you ever asked God something and he just said flat out No? He didn't say maybe, or later, or wait, he just said No. The creator of the universe, the one who holds the stars in place, provides for our needs and takes time to listen and answer us. When his answer is no, it is not one of hindrance or restriction, but one of discretion because he sees what we can not see.

In his omniscience, he resides in the future long before we get there. In his omnipresence, he surrounds us, leading us in a direction that is consistent with his will. In his omnipotence, he is mighty enough to handle everything including the situations of life.

God cares for us, loves us and wants the very best for us.

God cares for us, loves us and wants the very best for us. He desires our life's journey to be one full of knowledge and experience. He lets us know when we tread down the wrong path. When he says this, our job is not to battle with the decision, or question, it is simply to acknowledge our trust and dependence on him. This type of trust is only birthed out of a loving relationship with the Father in which He made the first loving move towards us.

There are prayers that God answers with a resounding YES! The yes means to move forward and advance. He wants to fully accomplish what he has set out for you to do. The yes he has given and task you have committed to will cause sacrifice in some areas of your life. You do know that God said to walk in it and this is assurance enough that everything will work out for your best good. In this, God will provide guidance, he will not lead you to handle the assignment of your life on your own.

God provides everything that we need in order to complete the journey that is placed before us. For example, you are preparing your child for a new school year. Would you purposely send him or her to school without paper, pencils, crayons, a book bag and lunch? You have an expectation of the child that involves success and going to the next level. As a result of this expectation there is unmerited provision. God is the same way. He would not prepare us for something, give us an answer to proceed and not provide everything we need to make the journey.

We must ask ourselves, will we try to make our own map or will we accept the map from the one that created the road?

Trusting God's answers is not always an easy thing because human nature gets in the way. Even in times when there is not understanding, we must trust and place our hope in God. In this we must get past what we physically see. We have the sense of sight in the physical realm, which becomes our reality. What we see determines what we will believe. It becomes a factor into what shapes our decisions prior to consulting with God. However with God what you see is not the end of the story. It is the unseen that we should believe.

Hebrew 11:1 says *"Now faith is being sure of what we hope for and certain of what we do not see."(NIV)*. What we define as certain are things that are readily identifiable to us in our boundaries of eye sight. If I can't see it, how can I be certain? Now faith is being sure of what we hope for. Having hope means to believe in that which has not come to pass yet, you have not began to see it manifest in the physical realm, but there is an assurance within that it will come to pass.

Hope is a privilege my friend. It is the opportunity to defy what we see in the physical realm and choose to believe and trust what God said. Hope is spiritual because it defies everything that our physical eyes can perceive. The one thing that he desires most from us is that we trust him. As God's children, the hope of glory is seen in us.

When we listen and trust God, we place our confidence in knowing that he will lead us where mercy resides, where his strength is our joy, where his provision abounds and where his grace is sufficient.

Many times we get caught up on what we want, our agendas or what we think is right. Have you ever walked up the wrong staircase to find an unintended destination? You made the ascent, you pressed through and stay the course, but it was not the right course. This is what God is trying so desperately to get us to avoid. He does not want us to go up the wrong staircase, he desires for us to ascend on the correct one. In order to avoid this from happening, we must commit our ways to God, seek his direction, and obey no matter the cost.

Serving God is the reason for living.

Serving God is the reason for living. It is not to fulfill our agendas while asking God to serve as our butler in accommodating us. His work is much bigger than anything our minds can conceive and we have to trust that he knows best.

This trust that I continually speak about is found in the experiences of life. They are the lessons, the trials, the happiness and the pitfalls we go through. While going through them, he promises never to leave us. Many times he carries us through. His desire is that we press and this is where faith abounds, our spirits mature and we learn that there is more to this life than our wants, plans and agendas.

God is growth and change. On our journey, we will experience growth and change constantly. Anything that is not growing and changing ceases to exist- it is dead. Life is always on God's mind, make a choice to live a F.R.E.E and abundant life by trusting God.

The Liberating Truth

Being F.R.E.E propels us to a place where liberation is experienced. We go there in our minds and spirits far before you arrive there physically. In some cases like those of the prisoners the physical freedom does not occur on earth, but in eternity.

We are all given the opportunity to choose mental and spiritual liberation. It defines who we are and who we are destined to become. Liberation ushers in a free flow of thoughts and ideas. Life becomes what it is intended to be and that is a service to God.

Freedom is not something that can be experienced in books, movies and various forms of media, freedom can be your reality, something you live for everyday, something you desire so much that you will not let anything or anyone to take it away from you.

Living the F.R.E.E life is not one that consist of existing without rules or restrictions, there are definitely some that are formulated along the way. These rules and restrictions serve as a form of government for life. Rules and restrictions do not restrict your F.R.E.Edom, they allow you to enjoy it fully. They serve as boundaries and guidelines, providing order for living. When the rules are observed, liberation is still present and there is an opportunity to freely experience the joy of life.

Paradigm of Patience

Waiting, waiting, waiting..........waiting. The word "wait" is quickly becoming a word of the past.

In the age of technology and instantaneous happenings and results, we are losing sight of what it means to wait. We want FAST food, INSTANT messages, and EXPRESS mail. As technology has evolved and changed rapidly, we have adapted to the environment of this change. Anything that takes longer than two seconds to formulate is dismissed as not being fast enough. Waiting has become nearly obsolete and undesirable. People, places and things have to stay on the move in order to stay relevant in our eyes.

I am no exception to this speed concept. Being that I was born in a technological era, my short life has seen its fair share of changes in technology: from Vinyl records, to cassette tapes to CDs to MP3s, the world has changed quickly. We have seen rapid progression in every industry over the past twenty years. Things are evolving, changing, reinventing themselves and speeding up on every front.

As we take on this mentality in the ever changing world around us, the mindset of this rapid and instantaneous mentality is applied to our lives as well. We want companionship instantly, friendship instantly, money instantly, and a new perspective on life instantly. Nothing in life seems to come fast enough.

As we grow and change throughout life, there has to be a change of mentality as it relates to patience and time. In order to get a new perspective of this, we must look to the originator of time, God.

God created time out of eternity, lets think about that for a moment. He took eternity, which is endless and created time within it. It is like having a large roll of flattened cookie dough and cutting shapes out of it that are shaped within a precise parameter. Time as we know it is part of a larger picture. It is a segment, just a chip in comparison to eternity. Eternity is vast beyond what can be imagined. Time and the life span of a human is a few moments as it relates to eternity.

Time is definable, containable and continuous. Time is something that was created by God in Genesis chap. 1, when he created the earth. He created the light and darkness, each having a specific time to dominate the earth. Gen. 1:2-5 reads *"And God said, "Let there be light" and there was light. God say that the light was good, and he separated the light from the darkness. He called the light "day", and the darkness he called "night". And there was evening and there was morning-the first day.*

This was the first day of time on earth. Prior to creation, there was only eternity, which had no definition in terms of day and night. So the definable contents of time were governed by the light and the darkness. The sun and moon were not created until the fourth day, thus light and darkness constituted day and night prior to us to having a symbol to justify them. This miracle was something only a creator could do, God defined time in our eyes and the evening and the morning are still governed by the light and darkness.

Taking a look at life and how God ordered it to be done in a process is very important.

Taking a look at life and how God ordered it to be done in a process is very important. As the days of the creation were completed, God did specific things on each day. When you have time, read just the first chapter of Genesis, which is a summary of what was done during creation. As we look at it closely, we can learn various things from it. The first of which is God created specific things on each day which was a part of His process. The creation of water, birds, sky, land animals, man and woman were all completed in order. Nothing on the earth was placed here prior to its provision being made. Creation was accomplished in divine order and at the end of the sixth day, it was complete and whole.

We can learn a valuable lesson by looking at creation and his order. The process by which he created the earth is the same process that he uses to govern our lives. We are not exempt because we can boil minute rice.

There is a divine process that we are all a part of and we must embrace a mindset of patience and…..waiting. There has to be a paradigm shift in our mindset about time and the process of it. Let's discuss a practical example to bring all of this together.

Icing on the Cake

Let's view the process from a practical perspective: baking a cake. The oven is preset to a certain degree, the ingredients are mixed together, the batter is beaten and prepared. It is time to place the cake in the oven. As the cake begins to bake, you take a look inside to see it begin to formulate into a delicious desert. The aroma of the cake fills the room and the scent entices your appetite as you anticipate the taste of the confectionary creation. The cake is shaping up great, you take a look in the oven and see the top becoming golden brown and it looks great. There is still time on the kitchen timer, but it appears to be finished.

In anticipation, the cake is removed from the oven and instantly, it drops. Oh my goodness, what happened? As it deflates the middle begins to ooze out of the side revealing that the batter that is not baked at all. Suddenly, the anticipation and expectancy of the cake is lost in a moment because the process was not complete.

Everything has a process from baking a cake to the activities of our lives. Nothing in life is exempt from the procedures and progression of events, known as process. Process serves a variety of purposes and without it recognizing development in your life becomes difficult. It is God's way of refining us, he sends us through process for our advancement and never our detriment. His order and process are unparalleled and unmatched in our reasoning of how things should happen.

Many of us neglect, try to deny or skip over this notion of process because society tells us to get it and get it now! Our minds have been shaped to believe that anything good has to come within a particular and reasonable time frame.

The lesson of what God is tailoring to teach you are in the confines of the process. If there is no patience in the process or a change in mindset as it relates to the process, we miss the point of the process. Is it really worth it to go through something and omit the process for the sake of seeking its end? The blessing of the journey is normally not located in its ends, but it is experienced along the way.

One of the reasons we experience the process is for the development of patience. I have heard people say, "I will never pray for patience", most people do not pray for patience because they do not want to PAY for patience. When patience is involved the process will cost you something. You have to be ready to invest in the process, it will definitely be worth it. It helps us look to and listen to God more clearly and allows us to determine what is being said to us.

Time is the requirement; it is your passport to patience. Understanding and insight come when we are patient with the process that has been set before us. These are very helpful aspects as it relates to process because they help make sense of what we are experiencing.

When we allow our mindsets to release the notion of a time restraint, we are open to experiencing a paradigm shift. Through understanding and insight mindsets begin to shift. Once we are removed from panic and "I can fix this myself" mode; our minds are relaxed enough to listen, process and react in a more sensible manner. A change of mind as it relates to waiting and patience is the way we conceptualize our process. Once this happens, we are able to adjust our lives to develop patience and seek peace in the midst of the process.

My friend, do the work that is required. You have God on your side, the very one that created time and has created a process for you. Utilize the process for your advantage because there is divine purpose and provision in it.

In Galatians 5:22, patience is listed as one of the fruits of the Spirit. Patience is a virtue that is given by the Holy Spirit. By nature, patience defies every instantaneous notion that we are accustomed to because it requires waiting and contentment in that state. The state of contentment when it comes to waiting is where process and patience take ultimate reign and you open your heart, mind and spirit to say to God, "I'm here Lord, teach me, process me, I am content with your process."

This state of patience is where we surrender our will to God, the control of timing and we begin to set our focus on what God has in store to teach us. What is so amazing is that as we surrender our will to God and relinquish timing control to him, he gives us a sense of peace and consistency with the journey. That is the best place we can possibly be because it places us at the center of God's will.

We become subject to his will, which is his ultimate purpose for us. At this stage we avail to what he is calling us to do. We can no longer try to make it work ourselves, we have decided not to pull the cake out of the oven and wait for the process to be complete.

Let's revisit the story about the baking process. The baker has gathered the ingredients needed to bake the culinary masterpiece. The oven is preset to the proper degree; he blends the ingredients together and pours the contents into the baking pan. As the cake's aroma fills the kitchen everyone that enters is greeted by it. The cake begans to take shape and the baker takes a glance into the oven, "ah, beautiful" he says to himself as he continues his work. The cake swells to display a golden, brown top and the aroma grows stronger. After a while, he walks over views the cake under the light and heat of the oven, "not yet", he says.

Forty five minutes pass, the baker finally opens the oven and removes the cake. It is complete, perfectly baked, stable and intact; the cake has reached its full potential. While the cake was baking, the baker prepared a special icing for the cake. The cake is whole, the process is complete and the finishing touches have been added to make the cake a culinary success.

We are those unfinished cakes my friend. We are creations of God, the master baker that knows just how long the process will take.

God desires our lives to be a success for all to see.

God desires our lives to be a success for all to see. When our minds and hearts are open to accept the process as a part of a divine plan, we greatly benefit from the experience.

There has to be compliance with his timing in order for the process to come full circle and function as it was originally intended. God's timing is different from that of man, as we trust God and display patience with the process, we benefit greatly from the means of the journey, not just the end. The process makes us who we are and contributes to what we experience in the future. After the process is complete, we grow and transition.

The point of patience is to find contentment to endure. Enduring the process brings out character and we can actually learn quite a bit about who we are during the experience.

Most of us are unaware of our full potential, what we possess inside is innately given by God and discovered during the process. When we go through the process and make it to our expected end, God has been working on the finishing touches the entire time.

Bringing it together

We have discussed experience from how God views humanity to the importance of patience and process. Through each one of these aspects we experience life. Our definition of life as earlier outlined is defined by growth and change. Where there is no growth and change, life does not exist. Each experience that we have on this journey contributes to a mature, prosperous and fully developed life.

I admonish you to view your life experiences from a new perspective, in which you look for lessons that each experience holds. It will truly liberate you to walk in the F.R.E.Edom that you were designed to have.

Through trust, patience and process, you will fully see how the experiences of your life are linked to your purpose. These aspects teach you to depend on God. Your process is designed to make you better, through it, your trust in God will grow and patience will grow. He desires to use your life for greatness and you are the very best vessel he ever created. Your experiences are useful for his service. Through this, you are liberated and F.R.E.E.

8

Expansion

Welcome to Destiny

Time for Action

Now you are standing at a pivotal point –a point of change, decision and development. The lessons of life's experience are before you like an open book. You are realizing that everything that surrounds you is a moment that is uniquely designed for a reason and purpose. Now you are ready to Expand.

Expansion is where the evidence takes place. It is where the fruit of what has been planted, grounded and cultivated within you begins to come forth. It is a place of movement. Previous thoughts, actions, and even your lifestyle become eclipsed by new thoughts, ideologies and habits that have become a part of who you are. As you develop into the person that you are called to be, miraculous growth is seen. What happened on the inside is seen on the outside. This growth manifests itself in a variety of ways such as positive thinking, patience, release of bondage, the conqueror's attitude and others detailed earlier in the text.

Expansion is the growth of your character; it is the maturing of your mind and the development of your spirit. The Expansion is where the changes culminate to form a beautiful picture of your F.R.E.Edom.

Expansion involves actively pursuing those things that you are called to be.

Expansion involves actively pursuing those things that you are called to be. At the Expansion phase, you are given the power to progress, conquer and effectively impact the people and circumstances around you. You have the power through God to accomplish great work.

Expansion is about living out the purposeful plan of your life, enjoying the fruit of life's lessons and living new. Expansion is where you understand that your journey and the experiences along the way have contributed to who you are.

You are purposefully made.
You are called to conquer.
You are designed for greatness.
You are here to E X P A N D.

What is in Your Hand?

The definition of Expansion literally means to stretch out. It also means to overcome that which surrounds you. Expansion is going beyond your abilities to do what is required in order for the glory of God to be seen. It is a point of transformation and realization that all things are possible. God used people throughout the Bible to liberate, develop and cause expansion in the lives of others. Moses expanded his staff over the Red Sea and the waters parted to form dry land leading the Israelites to liberation. Elijah stretched himself out on a deceased child and the child was resurrected. Jesus extended his arms in love on the cross and died for the sins of the world. In all of these instances, stretching was involved. The same way these people were used to exemplify God's glorious expansion is the same way he desires to use you today.

As children of God, our lives become renewed in Him. Ephesians 4:22-24 says "That ye put off concerning the former conversation the old man, which is corrupt according to the deceitful lusts. And be renewed in the spirit of your mind. And that ye put on the new man, which is after God is created in righteousness and true holiness." (KJV) This scripture declares that we have a new lease on life. It is an opportunity to be renewed in the spirit and put away those things of the past.

This, my friend this is the beauty of Expansion. It gives us the chance to move beyond the past to embrace new life. In that we have a responsibility to live according to the standards of this newness where all things are possible.

The renewed life is an opportunity to depend solely on God. Depending on God's renewing power sustains us against opposition because we understand that we are not achieving purpose on our own. Purpose and effective living are accomplished through God's power working in us.

We are equipped with spiritual gifts that are designed for purpose-driven use. Spiritual gifts are those things that God has given you be a blessing to others. Gifts are given with the intention to serve and give. The aspects of purpose, serving and giving summarize the effectiveness of Expansion. Unlike the world's viewpoint which is self centered, driven and focused, the F.R.E.Edom viewpoint is purpose and people centered, driven and focused.

Purpose driven acts are an outward expression of God's love for us and others.

Purpose driven acts are an outward expression of God's love for us and others. As God's children and instruments of purpose, we have the unique opportunity to serve as a part of the body of Christ. Accepting the Lord in your life is the prerequisite to a renewed life and equips you to embrace passion and purpose. We are given over to his spirit and likeness when we accept Christ and our spiritual gifts are stirred within us. We live out God's will for the body of Christ as we utilize our gifts.

The body of Christ is a group of believers working together to accomplish common goals. Within the body everyone has a function, a task and specific skill set that is used to move the Body forward and exemplify God to the world. The word of God says "Now ye are the body of Christ and members in particular." (I Corinthians 12:27 KJV). This is the primary goal behind Expansion.

His glory is revealed in us by having faith in Christ. When we begin to fully function the way God intended, we expand beyond what we could have ever imagined.

The kingdom of God functions in all efficiency of things because God empowers its citizens. Born again followers of Christ are cared for by God and his system of principles on earth and in eternity.

Development and Expansion

Expansion is multi-faceted and affects many areas of your life. Development becomes evident during Expansion. These two entities are coupled; one can not happen without the other. Development is defined as maturity in action. Expansion means to cover and stretch out. As Expansion is taking place in your life, development is simultaneously happening as well.

The way I knew I was experiencing Expansion in my life was when I started my first business. I was developing a mindset of ownership, as this took place, I was expanding my contacts, business transactions and presence in the market. My work as a consultant developed, thus my business expanded.

Development takes place in many forms: mental, spiritual, emotional and physical. It is contributing to the purpose that you are designed to fulfill. Development manifests one step at a time. These building blocks of your life have been designed to develop you into a mature individual. Experiences contribute greatly to development, thus impacting Expansion.

The values, morals and ethics contribute to the development of character.

Character is who you are when no else is around; it dictates what you will or will not do in a situation.

Character is who you are when no else is around; it dictates what you will or will not do in a situation. It is who you are at the fiber of your being. Character is not easily changed by the standards of the world or anyone else. The unique blend of life experiences, applicable lessons, and development into a mature person are contributing factors to character.

When you live an expanded life, God builds character within you through development. The spirit is developed by reading and studying God's word. The mind is renewed by its revelation knowledge and as a result the spirit develops and expands. You will come to know and understand your individual purpose as you develop. Romans 12:2 says, "Do not conform any longer to the pattern of this world, but be transformed by the renewing of your mind. Then you will be able to test and approve what God's will is-his good, pleasing and perfect will."

God gives us a fresh view on life and we begin to place our will aside and take on his perfect will. In his will, life is made full and we experience its abundance.

The word of God carries more meaning and depth as your spirit is developed by it. The word of God is an active tool that is most effective when it is applied daily. The word of God becomes alive and it is evident as the spirit develops and expands. It does not take a long time to grasp the principles and concepts of the word, but it is greatly beneficial to your development. Be intentional about spiritual growth by taking time to study God's word.

You are the Light

As we grow and walk in the light of a developed life, we reflect his light. The opportunity to reflect God's wondrous light is without a doubt one of the greatest gifts that we can ever receive. In John 8:12 Jesus speaks about the light of life: "Then spake Jesus again unto them, saying, I am the light of the world. Whoever follows me will never walk in darkness, but will have the light of life."

As we walk in the Expansion of God's light, it brings illumination to the darkness of our past. We can fully perceive our surroundings and allow development to take place.

Walking in God's light is a choice to walk in the truth.

Walking in God's light is a choice to walk in the truth. We change aspects of who we are to reflect the light in which we now walk.

God develops us so that his glory can be seen by others. The development that has taken place is not just for you, it is for the benefit of those around you. Take the time to share with others the development that you have experienced, someone can greatly benefit from it. Our command is to speak the words that the Lord gives us without fear because he has called us to speak with power, love and soundness of mind. This is growth in the light. This is F.R.E.Edom!

Expansion From the Beginning

And God said, "Let there be an expanse between the waters to separate water from water, 7: So God made the expanse and separated the water under the expanse from the water above it. And it was so. (Genesis 1:6-7 NIV)

In the beginning the area above the earth was called the Expanse. The expanse was the sky.

When we look at the sky from a ground view, we can not see an end to it. It covers the earth across the top completely from this viewpoint. This is the kind of expansion that God wants to give his children.

Our F.R.E.Edom in him should be wide as all the expanse of the sky. We are afforded the opportunity to be a part of an everlasting kingdom and serve a God that is much bigger, wider, and higher than ourselves. Just looking at the sky is a physical reminder of the greatness of our King. He owns the sky and allows us to stand under it, receiving all that he will shower on us. God did this very thing for Abraham, *"He took him outside and said, "Look up at the heavens and count the stars-if indeed you can you can count them."Then he said to him, "So shall your offspring be."* (Gen 15:5 NIV) God's promises are just this vast. He used the sky as a physical reminder of how great he was and how much he wanted to show Abraham. Likewise, he wants us to stand under a limitless sky and experience all that he has for us.

The expanse is where the stars hang, where the clouds shower the earth with the replenishment of rain and where the moon gives the earth light in the darkness of night. Just as the moon completes its purpose of lighting the earth, we are to serve the world as a light in the vast darkness of everything under heaven.

Expansion is never done quietly it always has a way of being recognized in some way. Your purpose is making an impact on those around you. As you expand, you will be placed in the forefront for people to see. Expect this as you develop in your purpose, it is what you are created for. As your light shines, it becomes a standard that all things can be measured and examined by.

Expansion Roadblocks

Expansion is a part of F.R.E.Edom, but there are roadblocks that hinder its manifestation in your life. In order for Expansion to flow in your life, roadblocks must be removed. Identifying the roadblocks is the first step; when they are identified you can move toward a viable solution.

One reason Expansion may not be evident in your life is because of unbelief and a lack of faith.

Faith characterizes our lives. *"And without faith, it is impossible to please God"* (Heb. 11:6 NIV). The absence of faith brings displeasure to God. Faith must be present in order for him to work on our behalf. If we do not see God's promise by faith, we can not recognize it when it manifests physically.

We must allow our spiritual insight to line up with the word of God.

We must allow our spiritual insight to line up with the word of God. As this is done, we expand in Faith and the physical manifestation soon follows.

Faith is an action word, which means it is doing, becoming and growing all the time. This, my friend is a form of Expansion. We are to become active in our faith.

Remember the Sovereignty of God and like Jeremiah 29:11 says, his thoughts are to prosper you and not those of harm. Take God's hand, show him your faith and he will assist you.

Ask God to increase your faith and what actions need to accommodate it. I'm quite sure there have been circumstances orchestrated to grow your faith. Ask God to allow you to reflect on some experiences where faith was the driving factor. He will show you if you are willing to see. You won't be disappointed.

Another reason why Expansion may not be taking place is because of disobedience. This one is deadly. I can not stress enough how important it is to obey. This requires fully obeying the complete commands of God. Disobedience is open rebellion. This is a quick way to stunt spiritual growth and delay Expansion.

In the book of Deuteronomy, God gave Israel a list of commands and the results of their obedience and disobedience of these commands. There was a very serious consequence for disobedience.

People choose to disobey for a variety of reasons. They maybe thinking, "this doesn't make sense", "this doesn't line up with my thinking", "this requires sacrifice". Whatever the reason I stress please, put it aside and do all that God has called you to do. Disobedience is not worth it, it will not compare at all to the Expansion that God desires to take place within you.

When it comes to making sacrifices, we all must do this in order to move forward. God is not trying to take from you; he is empowering you for Expansion. What you give out will surely come back to you. The principle of sowing and reaping does not only apply to physical attributes such as farming, finances or giving time, it is a spiritual principle that always produces a great return. When you place something near to your heart in the hands of God, it comes back greater, better and more wonderful than you could have imagined.

In Luke chapter 9, we find a familiar story of the two fish and five loaves. Jesus was ministering to a group of about 5,000. There was a child that gave Jesus his meager lunch. As he did this, the supernatural provision was made and all of the people were fed. Faith increased the sacrifice and all were blessed. In this same passage of scripture, Jesus said these words to the disciples:

"The Son of Man must suffer many things, and be rejected of the elders and chief priests and scribes, and be slain and be raised the third day. And he said to them all, if any man will come after me, let him deny himself, and take up his cross daily and follow me. For whosoever will save his life shall lose it: but whosoever will lose his life for my sake, the same shall save it." (Luke 9:22-24 KJV)

We must make a sacrifice in order to expand; it is in the sacrifice that we find the fullness of life.

We must make a sacrifice in order to expand; it is in the sacrifice that we find the fullness of life. Christ experienced Expansion when he rose from the grave conquering sin and death. He expanded in power to triumph over the sins of humanity and rescue us from a debt that we could not pay. His life was reciprocated to him when he gave up all for us on the cross.

Think about what it would be like if he did not go to the cross? If he decided to disobey, we would not have been able to experience the Expansion of our lives on earth to a life in heaven. Sacrifice is what Jesus' death on the cross was all about. He took our sins, when he was absolutely blameless and bore them for us. He sacrificed his life, is there anything greater than that?

This is how serious disobedience is to God. When we disobey, we cut ourselves off from Expansion. We also hinder others from experiencing the blessing of what God wants to do through us. The ability to reach others is the reason we are to obey in the first place.

God is always doing more than one thing. Obedience serves a dual purpose, one side is for Expansion, which includes growth and the other reason is for others to see God's glory and an example of a blessed life. In order to experience Expansion, obey, no matter the cost. It may not be easy, but it will be more than worth it. In order to experience Expansion, obey, no matter the cost.

The third reason why Expansion may not be evident in one's life is a lack of relationship. You have access to God when your life is renewed through Christ. The beauty and essence of a life centered in Christ is the benefit of relationship with him. A personal relationship with God is the greatest asset as a child of the king.

God hears you when you pray and most important he speaks back in a way you can understand. He gives instruction, leadership, wisdom and knowledge in all things. The path that we walk is made straight when we take time to build a personal relationship with Christ. He says in Proverbs 3:5-6 *"Trust in the Lord with all our hearts and lean not to our own understanding in all your ways acknowledge him and he will direct your path straight"*.

Trust is only present when relationship has been established. Where there is no relationship, there is no trust. If trust is absent the knowledge of his promises is not present. We experience the beauty of his love when we are in relationship with Him.

Cultivate a loving relationship with God. Expansion is one of the benefits and there are many that encompass your life to enhance you richly such as wisdom, knowledge and an understanding of God and his principles.

There are many promises throughout the Word of God that were placed there for us to expand in the knowledge of Him. It is up to us to read and stand on these promises. They serve as our equipment for living.

How can we know the promises if we do not spend time expanding spiritually in His word? There is no way we can, He says, the Word is our sword (Ephesians 6:17b KJV), it defends and protects. In Hebrews 4:12: "For the word of God is quick and powerful, and sharper than any two edged sword, piercing even to the dividing asunder of soul and spirit, and of the joints and marrow, and is a discerner of the thoughts and intents of the heart. (KJV)"

There are other Expansion roadblocks which include habitual sin, complacency, fear and unforgiveness. Pray and ask God to reveal to you if there is a hindrance that is holding up your Expansion. You are liberated in Christ and your experiences have been valuable teachers along life's journey. A roadblock will cause a setback to your Expansion, but it does not determine if you will finish the race. You have the power to conquer any roadblock that you face through the power of God. Remember, you are F.R.E.E through Christ and in him all things are possible.

Elevation and Expansion

There is something amazing about a bird in flight. When birds fly they function in the purpose that nature intended. When a bird takes flight, it rises quickly into the sky (expanse) gaining momentum from the wind around it. As its wings are spread wide, it begins to elevate itself in the sky and before you know it, the bird is out of sight.

We can learn a lot from this picture. Have you ever seen a bird try to fly with closed wings? This would not be a function that comes naturally to the bird and as a matter of fact, it is pretty much impossible for a bird to not fly without expanding its wings. As the wings are expanded, the bird can go higher and be elevated high in the sky.

When Expansion is present, it is accommodated by elevation. The two go hand in hand. Expansion covers horizontally, elevation covers vertically. As Expansion comes into your life, you are elevated and taken to the next level as well. Elevation is the act of being lifted, brought out and moved to another place. Elevation takes place spiritually, mentally, emotionally and physically, it is graduation from one level to the next.

Expansion and elevation allow us to be propelled by the supernatural force of God. He raises us up and sends us in the needed direction. He is our aviator. The force that he brings is not contingent on our strength, but is determined by him in accordance to the level of Expansion and elevation we are designed to reach. The elevation is the prize of the Expansion. God is the only one that can truly elevate us because he does it in the light of his favor and for the completion of his will. It is important to remember that as elevation comes, we take no glory of our own for the level we attain. The glory belongs to God because he has allowed us to be elevated.

Mindset of Expansion

There is a mindset that comes with Expansion. It is one that is free from the notions of lack, poverty, brokenness and inadequacy.

The mindset of Expansion calls for balance and stability.

The mindset of Expansion calls for balance and stability. To be balanced means to have order and equality in all aspects of life: spiritually, emotionally, financially, mentally and physically. Being balanced allows you to function in efficiency and maximize potential. When things are balanced, they are stable. Stability means to have your feet planted. This brings about an environment that is conducive for growth.

Expansion is where productivity takes place and where purpose is fulfilled. As Expansion and elevation take place, it is easy to lose sight of the driving force behind it. We must be very careful to evaluate the difference between God-purposed Expansion and self-willed Expansion. The two are very different and serve completely different purposes because one is self-centered and the other is God-centered.

God-centered Expansion reflects glory to God. It focuses on him as the foundation of the goodness you are operating in. Others see what he is doing through your Expansion and glorify him as a result. God-centered Expansion also involves supernatural power.

When God is the central focus of Expansion, he supernaturally provides for those that give him glory. This takes place through acts of unmerited favor, connections with people, and unexpected provision. God rewards us when glory is given where it is due. He does this to acknowledge our service to him and for others to be drawn to him as well.

Self-centered Expansion focuses on the goodness of self and how progression and success is a direct affect of personal actions. The glory is vain. Self-centered Expansion will do whatever it takes to get to the next level, including acts that are not in the will of God. There is no favor or provision in this because the basis of it is not God.

When the Expansion is not God-centered, we can not expect God's supernatural hand to in it. When we function in him, faith is activated and he is able to do things on our behalf that we could only imagine. The key to this is to let go of the self-centered focus and set our minds on the Expansion (and F.R.E.Edom) that God is seeking to provide for us.

Take for example the difference between two Israelite kings: Saul and David. Saul was the chosen by the people. He was elevated out of their desire for a king, as a result God honored their request and he ruled over the people. He did right in the sight of God for a while, but he began to become puffed up in pride and selfishness. He disobeyed God. Saul's self centered expansion begin to reflect in everything he did and as a result God removed his hand from him and the position that he had given him as king.

God's appointed king was David, the youngest son in the house of Jessie. He was the last to be considered, but he was appointed by God. David's character building and development started in the field with the sheep as a shepherd. God cultivated him in this position. David was elevated in the sight of God and the people during his kingship.

He brought honor to God and God's glory was reflected through him.

His experiences were chronicled through the hymns he wrote in the book of Psalms. These hymns are filled with admiration and praise to God that affected his life and the lives of those that read these scriptures. The God-centered Expansion that characterized David's life was seen by many generations. He became a man known after God's own heart.

These kings are examples of a difference in focus and mindset. One wanted to retain glory for himself, the other desired to reflect glory back to God. The mindset of Expansion requires an attitude of humbleness. The more you minimize the focus on self and reflect the glory to God the more expansive your life will become. Humbling yourself and placing your gifts, talents and treasure into the hands of God will cause you to expand and prosper greatly.

Our only focus is to keep the correct mindset. As we humble ourselves, acknowledge God, stay balanced and maintain stability we will see God's provision in our Expansion and beyond.

The Choice to Give it Over

God can be trusted with every aspect of your life.

God can be trusted with every aspect of your life. As you give it to him, he expands and enlarges what you have entrusted to him. This principle has allowed me to experience Expansion time and time again.

Give him whatever you are struggling with the most and allow him to take care of it in his wisdom, time and wholeness. Then the Expansion of rest and peace can enter your mind. Remember Psalms 55:22? *"Cast your cares on the LORD and he will sustain you; he will never let the righteous fall." (NIV)* By yourself, you can not handle it. Give it to the one that created it and allow him to handle it in the sufficiency of all things.

When you give God all of your concerns, you become lighter. As you become lighter, you are able to experience growth and Expansion. The lightness that you are walking in comes from laying down every burden and care upon the Lord.

Living without Regret

The choice to live in the Expansion of life is a choice to live without inhibition; which means to gracefully accept the present and have faith about the bright future that lies ahead.

When the Expansion is taking place, it is an enlargement of all that God has designed you to become. There will be times when the spotlight will be placed on you; those around you will be able to recognize the Expansion, the growth, the development and ultimately the elevation that has taken place in your life.

In the light of this fact, there will be critics on every corner. There maybe criticism that follows from ones that you may not expect. In this, please understand that everyone is not standing in your corner cheering for your Expansion. This can occur for a number of reasons. As long as you are walking in the will of God and you have not caused strife or contention with anyone, the problem lies with them and not you.

Expansion is a form of God-given favor. It is defined as something given to us that we simply do not deserve. At times, due to criticism or the actions of people we try to deny the Expansion that is taking place in our lives. We rather live under a rock in opposed to letting the light of Expansion shine through. Do not live in regret of anything that you are receiving from the Lord. He has given you what you have for a reason and you are experiencing Expansion for a purpose.

When we do not let our Expansion shine through, we are robbing ourselves and others of a ministering opportunity that God has designed to take place.

We Were Made to Connect

God loves relationship.

In the book of beginnings (Genesis) he created everything that we see in the earth and at the end of each day, he said "It is Good". God was satisfied with the work of his hand and he intricately designed it to coexist and connect together in the wholeness of nature.

In the midst of all of God's creations, when he created man, he said one thing about his existence, "It is not good for man to be alone." (Gen. 2:18a NIV) After this he said, "I will make a helper suitable for him" (Gen. 2:18b NIV)

Why do you believe that God would say this? God was relaying a very important point for all of us to see: we were created for relationship.

Expansion will require connection. The connections that are made along the pathway of F.R.E.Edom are strategically designed to serve a particular purpose.

Connections can happen in some very unconventional ways; however it is important to understand why you are being called to connect with certain individuals, organizations or groups. Being that relationships are important to God, he uses them to bless us and expand us. People serve purposes and most of the time the purpose is greater than what is recognized initially.

Connections are a large part of your Expansion. You were not meant to walk alone during this elevation point in your life. People will serve great purpose in your life; knowing and understanding this is a great benefit. Look for God to work in some very interesting ways in this area. Expansion is about realizing where you are going and allowing people to be instruments in order to help you get there.

Expansion is occurring all around you. It characterizes your future and contributes to the everlasting F.R.E.Edom of your life.

Remember, the Expansion is for the glory of God, not your own. You have arrived at this point for a reason that is larger than yourself. The glory of what is to come is much greater than what you have experienced in the past. People will see the Expansion that is occurring in your life and most important the Father has brought F.R.E.Edom to life through you.

9

Expansion

The Seven Benefits of Expansion

Expansion is a very tangible part of your F.R.E.Edom. It is where growth and development become evident. As you expand, you gain attributes along the way that serve as "the helping hands" to assist you as you reach for destiny and true purpose. Living the Finally Released to Experience Expansion (F.R.E.E) life presents an opportunity to gain positively from past lessons, recognize the gift of the present and looking forward to the promise of the future. This unique blend of benefits has been evident in my life and the lives of others that have chosen F.R.E.Edom.

We are privileged to go through the situations of life and gain positively from every experience we face. These benefits allow you to transition gainfully from one level to the next and develop into the person that you are called to be.

> *Expansion is a continual process that you will spend the rest of your life exploring as you live out F.R.E.Edom.*

Expansion is a continual process that you will spend the rest of your life exploring as you live out F.R.E.Edom. The Expansion of your destiny and purpose will continue to develop along the way.

As you grow in a holistic way and become cultivated in every area of your life, you will discover the Seven Benefits of Expansion. The seven benefits are Clarity, Wisdom, Direction, Strength, Affirmation, Soundness of Mind and Wholeness. These virtues become an asset to you and those around you. As you read through these benefits, recognize where they are evident in your life and utilize them to your advantage. As you grow and change, these attributes will grow and manifest in you as well. You will gradually go deeper and deeper into them as Expansion takes place.

Clarity

The first benefit of Expansion is Clarity. The word *clarity* is derived from the word *clear*. Clear is defined by Merriam-Webster as easily visible; plain; free from obscurity or ambiguity; easily understood; capable of sharp discernment, free of doubt, sure. As we discuss clarity, we will be able to see how possessing clarity lines up with this definition. Clarity is undoubtedly one of the greatest benefits of Expansion because it provides so much definition into where you are going and gives an aspect of vision that is recognizable and measurable.

The F.R.E.Edom journey is initiated by one's desire to find the missing element of his or her life: the link, the key, the purpose that they are living for. Looking for a deeper, more meaningful existence is how it begins.

At some point you may find yourself at a place that is not clear. Have you ever had a dream or vision that was not clear? At first, there is not much focus to what you see, but as you continue to look at it and process what it is, it begins to take shape in your mind's eye. Before long, you can see the picture clearly.

At the Expansion level, the development of vision is in motion and you have a good view of where you are destined to go. Clarity determines action. To know what you are called to do and why you have been through the experiences that you faced is a liberating notion within itself. At this point, one can begin to operate in purpose; operating at this level requires clarity. God will give you insight and vision into the destiny of your life, and vision will become clear. When you possess clarity, you actively take steps in a productive direction.

Confusion is the exact opposite of clarity. Confusion gives a distorted view of the future that causes one to aimlessly do things for reasons that are not beneficial or purposeful. Confusion is frustrating. It is a place of doing things out of emotion rather than reason and at the end can prove very time consuming and counter-productive.

When God began to reveal the true purpose of my life, I started to see that the activities of my life were not lining up with His will. I have always been the ultimate multi-tasker, jack-of-all-trades, it's just in my nature. Anything that someone asked me to do no matter how busy I was, I would find a way to accommodate their need. This left me in "go-mode" all the time, meaning I was exerting a lot of energy into things that were not very effective.

I was doing good things, running a profitable fashion consulting business, volunteering my talent and money for good causes, and serving in ministry at church. Good things right?

Were they lining up as the right thing? Not so much.

They were great things that I really enjoyed, but they were not the most effective things because they were not purpose-centered. They were talent centered. I was good at what I was doing, so I felt like that was "the call" on my life. This proved not to be the case for me. When my purpose became clear, it encompassed some of the skills that I was utilizing. I begin to put energy into activities that contributed to my purpose and I saw destiny unfold before me.

Clarity brings about the ability to properly prioritize.

Clarity brings about the ability to properly prioritize. This is a major part of your Expansion and F.R.E.Edom for a variety of reasons. Prioritizing means you do the most meaningful, effective things first and allow everything else to find its place in your life. The balance of this process is beneficial. It eliminates confusion and allows time to be maximized.

Time is one of our most valuable assets because it is so limited. How time is maximized is vitally important because it can not be replaced. No matter what measure of time we are talking about- be it a day, a year, or a lifetime-we must valuably utilize time.

When you learn to function in the benefit of clarity, you will see how productive and purpose filled your day to day activities will become. Purpose filled activities have eternal effectiveness and relevance. Eternal effectiveness goes beyond impacting the physical being, it is something that touches the soul, mind and heart. When we do things that are eternally effective, we make impacts on people that can change their lives and generations to come.

When clarity is present you can focus. Clarity brings about an opportunity to expand the boundaries of your capacity without adding more activity to your schedule. By doing the most effective things, you maximize your capacity of effectiveness, which allows you to accomplish purpose at an optimal level.

I can write an entire book on focus because it is something a lot of people wish they had. People claim ADD (Attention Deficit Disorder) at an alarming rate, they hold the notion that they can not focus. Focus is not a matter limited to the physical capacity. It is an aspect of spiritual awakening. Clarity enhances vision to see spiritual aspects clearly. Clear spiritual vision provides clear vision, which leads to staying focused on the purpose filled activities that will impact you and those around you. Focus allows you to set your sight on the end result even when obstacles are present.

For example, you have a vision of losing weight. Your goal is to lose 25 pounds. Even though this is a physical goal, weight loss starts with a paradigm (mental) shift from the inside out. The decision to lose weight is mental before it is ever physical.

So you start a workout regiment, begin taking vitamins and change up your diet. You are focused. You see yourself 25 lighter and living a healthy lifestyle.

As you begin to lose weight 5, 10, 15 lbs, your focus and drive to succeed become stronger. Those cookies and candy in the break room are no longer a temptation. Your weight loss goal is clear and will not be denied.

This kind of result can only be present when there is focus. Focus says, "The goal is in reach, continue to go for it." All of these attributes are wrapped up in clarity and as you benefit from this at the Expansion level, you gain more than you bargained for.

Wisdom

Everyday we make choices. We choose what we want to eat, how to arrange our daily schedules, what to wear, where to shop for groceries, what we are going to devote our time and energy to and on and on and on. With these choices comes the opportunity to make decisions. The way we know how to make a good decision or not is by using wisdom.

Wisdom is a benefit of Expansion because it allows us to make quality decisions. These decisions are important because they determine how time and energy will be spent.

Knowledge is derived from wisdom which comes through personal experience, listening and learning from the experiences of others, and it can be God given. In 2 Chronicles 1:7-12, we see a prime example of God-given wisdom. These verses chronicle a conversation between God and Solomon. God asked Solomon to request whatever he wanted and it would be given to him. This is Solomon's response in verse 9-10:

"Now Lord God, let your promise to my father be confirmed, for you have made me king over a people who are as numerous as the dust of the earth. Give me wisdom and knowledge, that I may lead this people for who is able to govern this great people of yours?" (NIV)

What a request ! Solomon asked for wisdom.

To desire wisdom signifies development because it is not a self-centered request. When we see further than ourselves and become self-less, we can request things from God that will not only be beneficial to others, but in turn will be a benefit to self.

God responded in 2 Chronicles 11-12:

God said to Solomon, "Since this is your heart's desire and you have not asked for wealth, riches or honor nor for the death of your enemies, and since you have not asked for a long life, but for wisdom and knowledge to govern my people over whom I have made you king, therefore wisdom and knowledge will be given to you."

Solomon determined that wisdom and knowledge were more important than anything else he could request in order to lead God's people.

The value that wisdom possesses is deeper than tangible things because it allows you to make decisions with power. Decisions made from a point of power are effective in the present and the future as well. Functioning in wisdom requires the ability to discern what is correct and not correct.

This is where knowledge comes into play. Knowledge is derived from the lessons acquired through experience. As we combine these lessons with God-given wisdom, we maximize our ability to make decisions.

The Book of Proverbs was written by Solomon and is known as a book of wisdom. Proverbs contains valuable advice as it relates to wisdom that can be applied to our lives today. Wisdom is timeless, it knows no bounds and to have it is more valuable than money, tangible things or anything else Wisdom brings about an aspect of being sound, meaning you are solid in your thinking and understanding. You are not imbalanced, but you are functioning in wisdom and it guides your decision making process.

In Proverbs 8, wisdom is personified and given a voice so that we can better understand it. Solomon wrote from this aspect to help us understand wisdom's attributes. Proverbs 8: 12-20 says

"I, wisdom, dwell together with prudence; I possess knowledge and discretion. To fear the Lord is to hate evil; I hate pride and arrogance, evil behavior and perverse speech. Counsel and sound judgment are mine; I have understanding and power. By me kings reign and rulers make laws that are just; by me princes govern and all nobles who rule on earth. I love those who love me, and those who seek me find me. With me are riches and honor, enduring wealth and prosperity. My fruit is better than fine gold; what I yield surpasses choice silver. I walk in the way of righteousness, along the paths of justice." (NIV)

As this chapter continues, it sheds light into wisdom and how it impacted creation. The chapter offers instruction and direction on what happens when wisdom is not present. Wisdom is a great thing to possess and when one has it they can benefit greatly.

The interesting thing about wisdom is that it does not always follow "the norm". What is wise is not always popular. Wisdom can go against our natural tendencies and thought patterns. However, it is useful and most of the time extremely beneficial to operate in wisdom even if what you are doing isn't the conventional thing to do. Making wise decisions can make all the difference in the world. Spiritual enlightenment and elevation increase when wisdom is present. It is an important tool that can guide, lead and offer insight when making life decisions. Yield yourself to the wisdom of God and watch the wonder of your future unfold.

Direction

When you have a clear picture of where you are going direction gives evidence of this. In order to go in the right direction, you must realize where you are headed. Even though we walk by faith and not by sight, we cannot move forward without direction. To know where you are going is a benefit of Expansion; to walk in the direction of purpose is a great gift. When we understand what is required of us, we can fulfill destiny.

To function with direction means there is not a lot of extra baggage to carry along the way. One of my favorite songs has a line in the chorus that says "pack light". When you are moving amidst the chaos of the world and those around you, you have to move with precision. Every step in the right direction is a step that holds value at the Expansion level. Extra baggage does not allow you to do this, carrying less in the form of mental, emotional and spiritual baggage is vital.

As you elevate in an upward direction, there are not a lot of people taking this way because it is not the most glamorous thing for you to do. However it is the favored thing and the one that will allow you elevate continually.

Moving aimlessly without direction or instruction for that manner is not very wise. Running from what you are destined to do and defying God's will only leaves you to repeat the cycle again and again. The Bible states in Psalms 37:23 (KJV), "The steps of a good man are ordered by the Lord: and he delighteth in his way." If the direction of your steps has been ordered, they will bring you to your expected end. Anywhere else may lead to the incorrect result.

There is nothing wrong with planning a course for your life, setting goals and living them out. However, it is always important to leave room for the unexpected. When we chart out our lives so much that we don't leave any room for God to work, he has a sure way of rearranging our plans according to his will.

The beautiful thing about the F.R.E.E journey is that you don't have to have all the answers.

The beautiful thing about the F.R.E.E journey is that you don't have to have all the answers. Sometimes you can only see the next step, not the complete road. Somehow you know that you are called to end up at the expected end. Trusting the one that gives direction causes the next steps to be made with boldness and confidence.

During the Expansion part of the F.R.E.E. journey, you maybe called to take a direction that seems unusual. You don't know why or even how, but trust, the steps were ordered. If you stand in confidence and go in the direction that you are called, you will not be disappointed.

"Trust in the Lord with all your heart and lean not to your own understanding. In all your ways acknowledge him, and he will make your paths straight" (Proverbs 3:5-6 NIV). This verse teaches us that trust is required. You must rely on God to give direction and not solely on what appears to be the right direction.

If you acknowledge that you don't have all the answers, it leads to dependence on the one who does have the answers. This also holds the promise of being directed on the straight path, meaning the direction is sure: there is no wavering or u-turns required. The beauty is that as we walk, we are increased.

When you go in the right direction, you experience favor. Favor is something that is unmerited, undeserved and most important, it is always on time. The open door of favor has not been opened by you and can not be closed by anyone else. When you operate in favor and you are living on purpose, people will assist you along the way.

At times they won't even know why they are showing favor to you, but it is a supernatural thing. Favor is not readily understood, but it is always what you need when you need it.

I remember when I was purchasing my first home, I needed the earnest money in order to make the down payment, and it was a matter of paying my tithe or having the earnest money when I needed it. I paid my tithe. The same day, I received a call from someone who told me God instructed them to give me a certain amount of money, which was the exact amount of the earnest money.

Countless people have experienced favor when they walk in the right direction. The beauty of favor is that it proceeds and follows. When you are going in the direction of purpose and destiny, favor will meet you on that pathway. God will equip others to equip you. Favor also follows you, meaning every step that you are taking has been a walk of favor and it is utilized to get you from one place to another.

When we take the right direction, we are glorifying God with our actions. We show him we are appreciative for expanding in purpose and being F.R.E.E by living out the destiny for our lives. We become recipients of favor as we live out our true calling.

You are at the point of Expansion to do just that—expand. Taking steps to get there requires faith. Faith without works is dead and I would also add that direction without steps is dead.

Mobilize your faith. As you walk, you will receive more and more direction as to where you need to go. It is ok not to have the entire map. We only need to place one foot (action) in front of another in order to move forward.

Direction is a benefit of Expansion, to have clarity and actually know what direction to pursue is something people spend their whole lives looking for. Searching is not uncommon, but when we have direction, it is vital to execute.

I have seen the benefit of Direction literally change the course of people's lives because they are no longer living out what they "think" they should be doing. They are living with purpose and dwelling in the land of destiny. They are living F.R.E.E. When we embrace the F.R.E.E life, we can live in peace with our purpose and move boldly in the right direction.

Strength

This aspect of Expansion offers endurance, perseverance and sheer determination. Strength acts as a spiritual backbone. When the back is strong, many things can be carried on it and most important, it holds up the frame of the body. Without strength in your back, you would not be able to bend, lift, pull or push anything and there is a loss of mobility. This is the same way strength positions itself in the spiritual realm as well. Having strength means you have what it takes to hold it together and mobility to move forward and accomplish it. It becomes the fuel that you need to live out the destiny and purposes found in Expansion.

In order to be F.R.E.E, you must possess strength to weather the opposition that is going to come against you. Opposition is coming like it or not, whether it is anticipated it or not.

As long as there is life in you, you will encounter opposition. When you operate in strength, you can endure it.

As long as there is life in you, you will encounter opposition. When you operate in strength, you can endure it. In order to stand against the opposition, you must have a strong spiritual backbone.

You must put on the aspects of endurance, perseverance and determination which guide you through the circumstances that occur at the Expansion level.

Gathering strength is like putting a bucket into a well. It can be drawn upon when it is needed. F.R.E.Edom offers you the opportunity to reflect on the circumstances of life and draw strength when it is needed. We can reflect on these things and rest in the fact that if it was there for us then, we will be able to find strength again. Strength is drawn from elements of the past while leading to the future.

Strength is a supernatural aspect that allows us to endure. Supernatural means that there is someone higher than self that is contributing to the natural that we operate in. Strength comes from God, plain and simply, he gives us his strength for our weakness and gives us those spiritual vitamins that we need in order to continue our journey.

I can recall a situation that involved my five month old niece. She experienced head trauma during an accident. As a result, she had a seizure that left her in a coma. The doctors were not sure if she would make it. My family stood strong in faith believing for her recovery. As we prayed for her, other people began to pray for her strength and the strength of my family. We relied heavily on the strength of God and acted on his strength daily. After 3 days the baby opened her eyes, two weeks later, she was released from the hospital.

My niece is now nine years old and living a happy and healthy life. This is a true testament of the power of God's strength. During this ordeal, my family and I held onto Isaiah 41:10, "Fear thou not; for I am with thee: be not dismayed; for I am thy God: I will strengthen thee; yea, I will help them; yea, I will uphold them with the right hand of my righteousness." (KJV)

As you go through circumstances that require strength, others are watching. Some are praying, some are spectating and others are wondering how you will come out. In each one of these groups of people, there is someone that needs to see you demonstrate strength. As you gain strength and endure what you are facing, they can be strengthened as well. Those that are praying will see their prayers being answered. Those that are wondering how you will come out will see that it is possible. Others that are spectators may eventually stop talking about you long enough to learn from what you are facing.

When we walk through situations of life and recognize that strength is needed, we can ask for strength in prayer. Praying for strength and being open to receive it can make a world of difference in the situations that we face.

Even though strength is a benefit of Expansion, we need to think about strength in all aspects, mental, emotional, spiritual and physical. The battles that take place in our lives, especially in our minds are strong and we must have a source of strength in order to overcome.

As believers in Christ, we have the promises of God's Word that strengthens us everyday. "But those who hope in the Lord will renew their strength. They will soar on wings like eagles; they will run and not grow weary, they will walk and not faint."(Isaiah 40:31 NIV) When we are depleted, we have a source of strength that is not our own. Do you know that there is nothing that is impossible for you? You are empowered by God to endure, persevere and win? There is nothing greater than to know that promise.

As you expand, keep going; keep pursuing those things that God has called you to. Run the course, you are strengthened to endure it. It will be well worth it as you expand and elevate into greater things. You can accomplish those greater things. It is possible. Anything is possible. You can depend on God's strength to carry you through anything that you face. The strength that is derived from running the race of purpose will bring you to your expected and expanded end.

Affirmation

Living the F.R.E.E life requires commitment to: accomplish goals, live on purpose and walk continually toward the destiny of your life. To live committed, you must firmly believe in the promise, goal or vision you profess. This is where the benefit of affirmation appears.

When you live in Expansion, you have not only experienced growth and development; you are living out these aspects in your life. It is not a matter of just saying it, there are actions that accommodate what you know.

To affirm something means to stand without wavering behind it. It means to believe in it without fail. Affirmation causes one to be steady and stable in their thinking so that nothing can shake it. When you are called to do something that is purpose-driven and faith-filled, affirmation becomes an important factor that gives you a boost of assurance.

One of the meanings of affirmation is to express dedication.

People have a way of being good cheerleaders to a certain point. They will go on the journey with you for a while, but may not make it to the end with you.

Even when you find yourself alone on the Expansion portion of the F.R.E.E journey, sometimes, you must encourage and affirm yourself. Dedicate yourself to your F.R.E.Edom, live it out and expand regardless of what people may do or say. This is an area that is difficult for some because it is more fun to have someone or a group of people to walk with. However, when they are not present, you must keep going in the direction that you are called to go.

Affirmation causes you to rise up and keep moving forward, whether there are cheerleaders on the sidelines or not. There are always people around when things are going well, but know and understand when they are not going well, expressing dedication must still be your response.

One of my favorite books is called the 5 Love Languages, by Gary Chapman. This book changed the way I look at communication with people and with God. I learned that words of affirmation is a love language, meaning that people need to hear words from others to affirm them and more importantly they need that affirmation to receive love from God as well. The Word of God is the deepest, most heart-felt letter of affirmation that we can read. When you are experiencing Expansion and embracing the F.R.E.E life, affirmation is necessary. It causes you to elevate to new levels and experience new things. This can be a little un-nerving and can cause some uncertainty, it is natural. However, when we have affirmation to give us that extra confidence, we can conquer anything.

Determination is affirmation personified. As you are affirmed, it fuels the desire within to pursue purpose and destiny. Determination means you don't stop. It only takes one word of affirmation—be it from God, someone else or even from something resounding in the soul—to keep the fire within burning.

I believe that God allows this so that you can realize what you have on the inside and what we already know about yourself. Don't think it arrogant or overconfident, when you know what you are called to do and you are on that path, keeping that in the front of your mind is a very good thing. When there is no one else to encourage you, it is ok to do so yourself.

There are also times when people will be placed in your life to offer affirmation. The beauty of it is they may know you and sometimes they won't. Countless people have given me words of affirmation and encouragement as I was writing this book. Many of them didn't know me, but they took an opportunity to share. I was greatly blessed when I received the words they offered.

Take time out during your Expansion to speak and receive words of encouragement and affirmation. We are given ears to hear, hearts to feel and mouths to speak. The exchange of affirmation keeps you in a position to give it and receive it. The power of your words and the words of others are important. What you profess you will possess.

Soundness of Mind

"For God hath not given us the spirit of fear; but of power, and of love, and of a sound mind." these words are found in 2 Timothy 1:7 (NIV). These opponents of fear serve as attributes to your Expansion. The one that we will hone in on is soundness of mind. If it is coupled with power and love, it must hold some pretty high stakes in God's eyes right? It definitely does.

The soundness of your mind, is like "Mission Accomplished", "Destination Found" and "Purpose Realized". It is not the end of the book, but the beginning of a new chapter that includes you living in harmony and most important being at peace with what F.R.E.Edom has brought your way.

While one is searching, the mind is like a raging sea making it is very difficult to have soundness, solidarity and peace. When you are F.R.E.E, especially at the point of Expansion, you have a picture of purpose, a foreseen direction and the wisdom to get there. The mind becomes sound and content with the process. What you are called to do will take a majority of your time.

Soundness of mind brings satisfaction. When you accomplish purpose, the work of your life is satisfying to you. For example, an attorney had a very successful practice in Florida. He spent years growing his practice, and his clientele included some very notable people. After 15 years as an attorney, he decided to leave his practice to open a fish market in the same Florida town he had practiced law. He said he decided to quit law because it was made him imbalanced and his satisfaction was found in fishing.

This story has played itself out time and time again. People will put down professions, people and other signs of success for happiness and a sound mind. Even if they are successful at these things, they will turn to meaningful pursuits that bring satisfaction. The satisfaction of living out Expansion adds to liberation. We are able to live and be as we are intended to be: F.R.E.E.

The satisfaction of doing what you are purposed to do outweighs any measure of success that you think brings happiness.

The satisfaction of doing what you are purposed to do outweighs any measure of success that you think brings happiness.

No matter how big or small it appears to be to people, if we are called to do something, we will be satisfied with doing it. That does not mean our whole lives will be spent doing the same thing. Finding purpose is the beginning of the F.R.E.E life, you glorify God and bring yourself satisfaction at the same time.

Knowing your direction, having clarity and keeping your mind in a stable state allow you to make purpose-driven, forward thinking, productive decisions. These decisions lead to purpose-driven, forward thinking, productive results. This is exactly how you were designed to operate. Possessing a sound mind will allow you to journey through anything; no road will be too difficult for you to overcome.

Keeping a sound mind is not always an easy task. The appearance of obstacles and circumstances can be daunting; however the soundness of the greatest battlefield of all times (your mind) does not have to be subjected to those feelings.

Remember, you are at the Expansion stage which brings about an elevation of your mind. Elevate above whatever you see, see more than what is there and know that it is contributing to your Expansion in one way or another. Stay in balance, in harmony with your mind and nothing will be able to stop you from fully stretching out into all that you are destined to conquer.

Wholeness

Broken. Fragmented. Torn. Divided. This describes everything that is the opposite of wholeness and sadly most of us can identify with one or more of these descriptions.

What is wholeness? To be whole means to be complete, intact, unmodified and restored.

When we think about wholeness, we must start at the beginning with God. He is wholeness personified. The completeness of his being, the vastness of his character and the splendor of his work in creation demonstrates his infinite wholeness. Everything that he made fits together perfectly, in nature and in our lives.

When we look at the wholeness of nature, we see how plants and animals support one another to create an ecosystem that works harmoniously to keep the world in balance.

God is a three part being: the Father, the maker of mankind, the heavens and the earth, the Son, who walked the earth in the flesh and the Holy Spirit, which lives in us and works through us. Three is the indivisible number. The wholeness of God is seen in our existence as well. We are like him as spirit, soul and body. These three parts make up the complete being.

We were designed for wholeness. As we expand, we come closer and closer to all three parts residing in a harmonious manner. When we live out eternal purpose, the soul is satisfied, the mind is at work in a proactive, productive manner and the body can fulfill the necessary steps on earth. All three of these demonstrate the way wholeness becomes evident in our lives. In this, we function as the three-part being that we are.

Every miracle and act of God always has a whole result. Whether this is miracle that is found in the Bible or whether it was something that happened to you yesterday, when God shows up in a circumstance of your life, he handles every circumstance in complete wholeness. There are no question marks at the end of the day. Healing is accomplished in complete wholeness. When Jesus healed people's physical ailments, he addressed their spirit and mind as well. These were acts of complete wholeness. When we live in this, we have a more balanced life.

Expansion is functioning at a full capacity. This takes the devotion of your complete being.

Devoting your complete being to accomplishing the purpose and the destiny of your life will impact all of the levels of your life.

Devoting your complete being to accomplishing the purpose and the destiny of your life will impact all of the levels of your life. As you walk through the situations of your life, you will utilize energy from your mind, spirit and body. It will affect you on multiple levels. Wholeness is the same way. The elements that have comprised your life come together and construct the mosaic of your life, which is a diverse and wonderfully vivid picture. When you are whole, meaning nothing is fragmented, you become a picture of completeness.

Expansion carries the benefit of wholeness because you realize how the situations of your life are linked together to propel you into purpose and destiny. The desire to be whole demonstrates growth within itself because people that do not see anything wrong with the brokenness of their lives do not seek or value wholeness. There must be a level of readiness in order to find wholeness. We will spend a life time becoming whole and the elements that contribute to our wholeness liberate us.

Being complete-un-fragmented, un-broken, un-shattered—defines a prosperous life. Most think it is about money, but that is just the beginning. Having the body, mind and spirit functioning and moving in the same direction is the embodiment of prosperity.

When you do what you are called to do, you are F.R.E.E and that is prosperity. Prosperity is wholeness and allows you to lead a life of expanded totality. Functioning in totality allows you to utilize all that you have been given to purposefully accomplish your mission on earth. As you expand allow wholeness to encompass your life, it is yours to embrace. Live it, breathe it and become it.

The Seven Benefits will vary from person to person, experience to experience and elevation to elevation. As you live in F.R.E.Edom, spend time cultivating who you are. God has made you uniquely and perfectly to function in liberation from stereotypes and the standards of others. Your F.R.E.Edom is uniquely yours. Live this out as you journey and utilize the benefits of Expansion to elevate you higher and higher. Your life of growth and change will greatly reflect these benefits. Your character and the virtue of who you are will expand as well.

10

Live New, Live F.R.E.E

Throughout this book we have transcended through many defining moments. We have categorized these moments in a way that contribute to the purpose of life.

We have defined the Finally moment as a breaking point that initiates the F.R.E.E journey. We've walked through Release, which is a time of separation and letting go of those things that are not conducive to your journey. We have identified the purposes of Experience–the reasoning behind what you go through- and analyzed the experience in order to extract a valuable lesson. We have discovered that experience whether it is good or bad is linked to the purpose of your life propelling you toward the real reason for your existence. Last, we defined Expansion where you begin to live out greater purpose for eternal effectiveness. We have pinpointed the Seven Benefits of Expansion and how to utilize them in order to continually lead you along the F.R.E.Edom journey.

The F.R.E.E journey is a life-long course.

The F.R.E.E journey is a life-long course. We will spend a lifetime going through the peaks and valleys of the journey and learning every step of the way. There is always an opportunity to grow, change, and develop leading to a greater place of existence. Life is a cycling journey of experiences that are constantly elevating us and the benefit of every experience is something that we can look forward to.

Awakening

Some call it a realization, others call it an epiphany, I call it an awakening. An awakening is an eye-opening moment that causes life to be viewed in a different light. At the awakening point a stirring stimulation takes place. Dreams, passion, meaning of life and purpose wake up within you. Life is mobilized at a greater pace. What you were previously unaware of becomes blatantly obvious.

An awakening causes you to be energized in every area of life: physically, emotionally, mentally and spiritually. As these areas are affected, you are empowered to do wonderful things. The present and the future become opportunities to do God's will in every area of life and most important to impact others through completing purpose.

An awakening brings a charge of energy and commitment to the purposeful work that you are called to perform. Philippians 1:6 reads: "Being confident of this, that he who began a good work in you will carry it on to completion until the day of Christ Jesus." God is committed to completing the work he began in you.

The awakening serves as the enlightenment needed to lead you to a place of service. It will encompass your passion and cause eternal impact. When you are doing what you love, it does not feel like work, it is a delight because you are called to function in it. Arriving at this point is priceless and your life will never be the same once you encounter it. Awakening causes you to dance to the beat of your own drum. Embrace your awakening and live in the F.R.E.Edom that characterizes who you are.

Walk into the Sun

After the awakening has taken place, you will walk in the light of new found knowledge. Knowledge is important because it serves as a light that guides the destined path of your life. Being aware of this light will cause you to reside in a place of mental, spiritual and emotional illumination. Your life and the experiences of it are the reflection of an orchestrated plan that has led you to this very place and time. When you are illuminated, you carry the light regardless of the surroundings. Surroundings do not dictate how bright the light will shine and whom it will touch. It is only responsible for shining and reflecting the source of its being.

One morning I was driving to work. I took a different route in order to get there because of traffic. On this route I had to pass some places that held bad memories for me. The street that I was on was directly aligned with the rising sun. As I drove, I could barely see in front of me. I heard an internal voice say, "keep looking at the sun". I took my eyes off the road and looked directly at the sun, I was only able to see the course in front me, but it was completely clear. The places that brought bad memories were blocked out of my sight by the sun.

This story was so powerful to me because as I maintained focus on what was most important, I had clear sight on the path I needed to go. The point was that I kept my eyes on the light. As a result of focusing on the light, my path was directed straight and I made it to my destination.

In every situation that we have, we can choose to focus on the illuminating light which guides us every step of the way. You have begun a wonderful journey. Continue to look forward. Letting go of the bad memories of the past make way to the beauty of the future. Walking backwards will never allow you to see the horizon of promise. We must walk boldly in God's promise.

Throughout the Bible, God gave encouragement to the people he used to accomplish great things. He told them: "Be of good cheer", "Be courageous", "Do not be afraid". He was saying these things because he knew in that in their human frailty they would resort to feelings of doubt, fear and incompetence. The same way God spoke to them, he speaks to us today.

He wants you to accomplish those things that he has planned through you. God made a promise in Joshua 1:5 never to leave you or forsake you. He also gave you the promise that everything is possible with him. It doesn't matter what the inadequacy is or how impossible it looks, you are designed to win. Victory is yours and as his work in the earth is accomplished, we will be liberated to experience the joy that he brings when the work is complete.

No one has your set of experiences; they are uniquely hand crafted for you to learn, grow and develop. God had you and your experiences on his mind from the beginning of creation. You are designed to be alive for such a time as this. It is all a part of his orchestrated plan for you to live in the way of F.R.E.Edom.

Now that you can see how your life has been affected by your experiences. What will you do with the lessons? You have a wonderful opportunity to live in the light of this and never, ever return to the bondage of the past.

Your life is about living in newness and wholeness.

Your life is about living in newness and wholeness. You can truly be made whole if you decide to rely on God to make it possible in your life. He wants you to live a life of F.R.E.Edom in totality. Make totality your life long goal. Living new is a great place to begin.

The way you live new is to allow God to shape you and apply life's lessons to your present and future. A mind that has experienced Expansion can not go back to its former realm of thinking. Once you have experienced an elevation by God, it will not be of value to yourself or others to return to where you were.

F.R.E.E Now What?

Each time you encounter an experience that elevates and awakens you, it is time for action. These simple things have assisted me in making the activities of my life purpose-driven and meaningful. These practical ways of exercising F.R.E.Edom can be incorporated into your life on a daily basis. They are sure to make your journey enjoyable.

Share

Giving is a very large part of God's character. God is always giving to humanity. He gives us all of the beautiful things on the earth to enjoy. He gave his son who died for us in order to pardon our sins. He loves us enough to continually provide for our needs. We are charged to give as the Lord gives.

God is continually blessing you. Blessings are more than a raise in a paycheck or a healing that came for a family member. Blessings encompass all of your life they provide what you need in order to be F.R.E.E.

Every part of your journey has been designed with blessings to meet you right where you are.

Every part of your journey has been designed with blessings to meet you right where you are. They are there in the times they are needed most and God always knows what we are in need of. He doesn't leave us in a position to figure it out for ourselves, we are given his blessings in order to continue to journey and offer provision to those in need.

You are blessed for your life to be a display of God's blessings. Many people are broken, lost, without hope and wishing that someone would assist them along on their difficult journey. You are empowered with a testimony of God's blessings to encourage, strengthen and inspire people. By sharing you assist others in reaching F.R.E.Edom.

Sharing can be done in many forms; it could be through the sharing of time, advice, prayer, or financial support. The key is to find ways to share your experiences. You are a vessel. When you share it allows you to be utilized over and over again. Sharing also allows the blessings of life to be returned to you. When you do this, you experience the best that this life has to offer.

Make an Impact, Be the Difference

Living F.R.E.E is refreshing. It brings about new ideas, dreams and goals. The main goal of F.R.E.Edom is to live with purpose. Living with purpose affords you the opportunity to make an impact on the world around you.

You may not be saving the world on a daily basis, but you can positively impact the world in small ways daily. Some people find volunteering reward. Others utilize their skills and professional occupations to help others. In order to make an impact, you should identify an area of need that you are passionate about and start making a difference there.

Tanisha, a dear friend of mine volunteered for a holiday dinner outreach for the homeless a few years ago. While she was volunteering, she paid close attention to several adolescent girls that were at the outreach. Her heart went out to them and she became passionate about helping adolescent girls through their transition from childhood to womanhood. She decided to start a non-profit for youth called C.H.A.R.M.S: Cultivating Healthy Ambitious Multifaceted Sisters. Tanisha says that her life has become more fulfilled by living on purpose and impacting the lives of youth. She is truly making a difference in the lives of young girls and embracing the F.R.E.E call.

Making a difference is just a matter of passionate pursuit. Being passionate will propel you into action. This is a simple way to exercise F.R.E.Edom, but it is sure to make a world of difference in someone's life.

Move with Purpose

Everything that you do should be done with purpose in mind. Your actions should be meaningful and productive. This ensures that you are living purposefully and moving with efficiency. Before you make a decision for action, ask yourself: Is this activity productive? Is the action beneficial to me? Does this activity contribute to where I am going? If the answer is no to any of these questions, it is wise to reconsider the action.

Decisions that we make will have effects. It is up to us to determine if we are making meaningful decisions or ones that are not so meaningful. Moving with purpose takes reasoning into account. Act with a reason behind what you do. You would be surprised how activities will fall off of your list when you view them from a purposeful perspective.

Purpose will shape who you are and the individual you desire to be. As I came to realize my purpose, my personality began to change. I became conscious of my actions and how they would affect the image that I wanted to portray to the world. I thought more carefully about the activities I was involved, the places I went and why. When those things did not add up, they became a part of my past.

Purpose will govern your life. The desire to perform the most meaningful task will take precedence over other priorities. Your purpose will move you and be the driving force behind your actions and your restraints. Remember your actions are for the greater good and you will benefit greatly from this way of thinking.

Set Goals

You understand purpose. You are F.R.E.E and ready to move forward. One of the most important things that you can do is set goals, it is absolutely vital. A combination of short term and long term goals give you a working plan of action for your vision. I set goals in 30, 60 and 90 day increments. Setting goals on a small scale helps me accomplish them within a definable period of time and see progress quicker.

As you set goals they should be realistic, measurable and timely. Realistic goals are practical and attainable. Setting and attaining goals that are realistic help you define your accomplishments and what you need to do in order to reach the next goal. Measurable goals take into account your actual progress. It answers the question of how much did this goal help me get to the next level. Timely goals are set within a specific timeframe and give you something to consistently work toward. All three of these characteristics make goals easier to set and practical to accomplish.

As you reach your goals, do not stop there. Set another as soon as you accomplish one. This will create a pattern of progression. You will see the fruit of your labor when you progress and grow within your purpose. Your work will begin to come alive and you will be motivated to accomplish more.

Anticipate an Attack

As you live F.R.E.E, there will be people that do not like your progress. Everyone will not be a cheerleader for your success and people will slander you. It is important to remember and prepare yourself for this reality. People lash out against others for different reasons such as envy, jealousy, anger, misunderstanding and many others. If you mentally prepare yourself for attacks on your character and/or creditability, it is easier to handle when it occurs.

The most effective way I have found to counteract an attack is through controlling my emotions and keeping a positive attitude. I pray for individuals that come against me because I know it is just a tactic to get me off course. You must understand that the opposition does not want to see you win. When you are aware of this you are more likely to take your eyes off of them and focus on accomplishing purpose.

Maintain your F.R.E.Edom.

Maintain your F.R.E.Edom. You do not have to subject yourself to someone else's bondage. Take a stance on how you will respond and do not let others control your emotions. People only have as much control as you give them. Pray about keeping a positive attitude and disposition. This will empower you to conquer the attack.

Dream Big

This final piece of practical advice means actually what it says: dream big. F.R.E.Edom is yours. As you embrace it, you must dream the impossible. Your dream seeds are important to your purpose and were given to you by God to accomplish. You have to dream and imagine the impossible because anything is possible with God.

I enjoy spending time dreaming. Thinking about the future and how I would like it manifest in my life has motivated me to action many times. There are several ways to bring your dreams to reality. First, write down your dreams. Take time to put your dreams on paper. It is easier to obtain a dream when you can see it. It also gives you something to profess. What you profess you will process.

Second, create a visual description of your dreams. A visual description of your dreams is called a dream board. It is a combination of pictures and words that represent what you want to have. I love creating dreams boards because the possibilities are endless. It is your dream and you have full creative rights to make it what you want it to be. Place your dream board somewhere where you can view it often. The more you see it, the more it will become reality to you.

Last, pray and act on your dreams. You were not given these dreams to hide them under away or tuck them in the closet. Ask God about practical ways to bring them to life and act on what he says. Remember, small steps make all the difference. Whatever motivates you to make them come true is how you should act on them.

Strive for Greatness

I call this the passionate pursuit. In all you do always strive for greatness. Perform all of your actions in excellence. The presence is excellence can not be denied. It doesn't matter whether the meaningful action is large or small; execute it in a great way. Everything you do should be done well with honesty and integrity. Be true in your dealings with people and this characteristic will proceed and follow you.

Make excellence a standard in your life. When you do this, excellence becomes your expectation and you accept nothing less of yourself or those around you. People will recognize this and be charged to hold themselves to a higher standard.

Your good name and reputation is all you have. Your words and actions symbolize greatness. People will come to know what resides inside of you by the way you handle yourself and others. This liberating truth leads to the legacy of your life. Legacy is what people say about you when you are not around and it is what they will remember about you after you are gone. Leaving a legacy of greatness allows your reputation to be seen in a good way and it has affects on the generations to come. This is how you make an impact on the world that can never be erased.

Living F.R.E.E accomplishes these things in you as you strive to live out the purpose you were created for. Let this characterize your life and it will become your guide to accomplishing great things.

Epilogue

We have discovered what it means to be F.R.E.E. I pray that you are encouraged to live purposefully. This book has led you to a decision making moment that calls for action. This very personal and unique journey is yours for the taking. Every step you take is leading to a higher place. I pray that you will live a life dedicated to fulfilling all that you are designed to accomplish.

Remember F.R.E.Edom is a process. You are making progress toward it everyday. You have overcome in order to be at this very moment and it is designed for your success. You are not defined by your past. You are designed for liberation from it. Shine in the light of God's glory and always live the purposefully, liberated life that belongs to you.

The F.R.E.E journey is a daily practice. I have written a short study guide to assist you with incorporating the F.R.E.E principles into your life. The purpose of the study guide is to reinforce the content of the text so that it becomes practical and realistic. There are fill in the blanks, practical questions, group activities and questions for group discussion. I encourage you to actively engage in applying the F.R.E.E principles and enjoy the journey that God has set before you.

"Live New, Live F.R.E.E"

Study Guide #1

Understanding F.R.E.Edom

What are the four stages that represent F.R.E.E?

F: _____
R: _____
E: _____
E: _____

What did you gain from reading the F.R.E.E introduction?
_____
_____

What insight did it offer?
_____
_____

Review the two foundational scriptures of F.R.E.E

Romans 8:28 (NIV) "And we know that all things work together for good to them that love God, to them who are called according to his purpose."

What does this scripture mean to you? _____
_____
_____

Study Guide #1 Understanding F.R.E.Edom

What does this verse say about your experiences and your purpose?

_____
_____

Jeremiah 29:11 (NIV) " For I know the thoughts that I think toward you, saith the Lord, thoughts of peace, and not of evil, to give you an expected end."

What thoughts does God have toward you? _____
_____
_____

How do God's thoughts toward you affect your expected end? What do you believe about your expected end? _____
_____
_____

Fill in the Blank:
F.R.E.E's Main Point:
Taking a look at the _____ will allow you to discover how the events of your life are _____ to the purpose and destiny of the future. You will look at how the _____ of your journey through fit together to form the "big picture" of life. Through experiences _____ _____ are learned that can be utilized for passionate, purpose driven _____ .

Group Discussion Questions

1. Name one experience that has taught you a valuable life lesson.

2. What hobbies do you enjoy?

3. How has your relationship with God shaped and guided you toward purpose?

4. What does being liberated mean to you?

5. How can you express thankfulness to God through your life?

Study Guide #2

A Moment of Change

A Finally Moment is a turning point, a moment when you say "enough is enough".
When did you decide enough is enough?
_____
_____

How do you feel that you are making strides toward advancement?
_____
_____

What are the Four Attributes of a Finally moment?
P: _____
E: _____
A: _____
R: _____

Fill in the Blank:

_____ and _____ are correspondents in the Finally stage of becoming F.R.E.E. What happens and when it happens are two very powerful _____ when it comes to embarking on the _____ journey. Timing will allow you to _____ the moment at the correct time and function in it _____.

Group Discussion Questions:

1. What changes did you decide to make when you found yourself at a breaking point?

2. How does viewing the reality of situation help you handle it better?

3. When you faced challenges of the past, did you feel prepared for them?

4. How did your Finally moment bring out the best in you?

5. How did you see God's hand in the Finally moment(s) of your life?

Study Guide #3

Points from a Powerful Perspective

How do you feel that your negative thoughts and words have affected you and others?

_____

_____

How can you change negative thinking to positive thinking?

_____

_____

What does God say about me?
   a. I am Loved: God loves me because of this I can love myself and others John 3:16, John 10:11, Isaiah 43:3-4, Deuteronomy 7:9
   b. I am Free: God has freed me; I am not a prisoner to my past or other people. Psalms 146:7B-8, John 8:31-32,36
   c. I am the salt of the earth: I am here to make a difference and produce good fruit Matthew 5:13
   d. I am a light for the world to see Luke 8:16, John 8:12, 2 Corinthians 4:16-17

Activity:
In order to help us discover meaning behind the words we say and what we think about ourselves take the letters of your name and write a descriptive word to represent each letter.

Example: ALEXIS: Awesome, Liberated, Elevated, eXcellent, Inspired, Spiritually Minded

Group Discussion Questions:

1. How do you exercise positive thinking?

2. How does negative thinking affect your activities and outlook on your experiences?

3. Why is it important for your thoughts to line up with what God has to say about you?

4. How do relationships play an important role in your thought process?

5. What choices will you make to remain positive in negative situations?

Study Guide #4
Destined to be F.R.E.E

As you cycle through the changes of life, you will have to let go some people and things in order to go to the next level. This stage is known as Release, it is a necessary part of your F.R.E.E journey. As you change your mindset and surroundings, the people around you will change as well. This may cause a range of emotions within you.

Name a person, place or thing you had to release in order to break the cycle in your life?
_____
_____

In what ways are you progressing during Release?
_____
_____

Fill in the Blank
God is doing a _____ _____ in your life. Embrace the _____ walk, the time is _____ for your F.R.E.Edom to be complete. In time your mind will be _____ and rejuvenated. You will find _____ to continue on your journey. If God has spoken to you about being _____ and progressing rest assured that he has _____ you to handle the solitary portion of the journey.

Writing Exercise
Release moments cause us to depend on the sovereignty of God. We must trust that his thoughts are higher than ours and in the happenings of our lives that he knows best.

Write a Thank you letter to God expressing your gratitude of his great work and plan in your life. Use examples of your release moments and what you have learned in the process, acknowledge and thank him for his work.

Group Discussion Questions:

1. How do you find contentment in a situation that seems to have no escape?

2. What are the three major ways God communicates to us?

3. Share an experience of God's perfect timing

4. How do you accept the letting go process; graciously or reluctantly?

5. Describe your personal moments of alone time. What lessons have you learned from solitude?

Study Guide #5

From the Pit to the Palace

Be it physical, mental or emotional, bondage creates a prison. These restraints construct walls in your life; nothing can come in and nothing can go out.

Activity:
Make an "X" in the middle of the box and write in each smaller area the "walls" that have been holding you bound. Outside of the bondage box write four words that are opposite of the words you placed inside. From today forward, live outside of the bondage box.

```
┌─────────────────────────────────┐
│                                 │
│                                 │
│        BONDAGE                  │
│                                 │
│                                 │
└─────────────────────────────────┘
```

Group Discussion Questions:

1. What can you do today to break the repeat offender cycle in your life?

2. What are the driving factors that make you unstoppable?

3. How can you display your faith to others?

4. How do you think your release fits into God's master plan?

5. What does it mean to be a new creation? (Refer to 2 Corinthians 5:17)

Study Guide #6
Life's Puzzle Pieces

4 Reasons for Experience:

1. To point out a strength or weakness.
Evaluation of character is defined what do you have on the inside. What is your strongest character trait?

_____
_____

2. Define a moment of triumph where a decision is made to win or lose.
What are you willing to fight for? Will you be defined or defeated?

_____
_____

3. Give you a testimony. There is no testimony without a test.
Identify an experience that gave you a testimony.

_____
_____

4. Allow us to learn the characteristics of God.
What have you learned from your experiences with God?

_____
_____

From Victim to Victory, the first three letters of these words are the same. You have a choice to be a victim of circumstance or have victory over it.

How have you been a victim in the past?
_____
_____

How can you have victory moving forward?
_____
_____

Group Discussion Questions

1. How have your experiences contributed to the person you are today?

2. How has your past set the groundwork for your future?

3. How have you grown stronger in an area of weakness?

4. How will you use your experiences to help others?

5. How will having a F.R.E.E perspective affect your future?

Study Guide #7

The Lesson Within

Trust and Experiencing God: We must believe that God has the best plan for us and not ourselves.

Define Trust
_____
_____

In what three ways can you trust God more?
_____
_____

Ways to Trust God
1. Trust his answers: his way is the best way. If he says yes, no, or wait it is for a reason.
2. Trust his timing: he works all things together for good and the timing is always seasoned to perfection.
3. Trust his abilities: he is ever present, all knowing and dedicated to your success.
4. Trust his word: He can accomplish through you those things that seem impossible. God will reassure you of his promises and his word. Reading his word will build your trust in him.

Fill in the Blank

God is _____ and change. Anything that is not _____ and changing ceases to _____-it is _____. Growth and change _____ life.

Group Discussion Questions:

1. Look at the events of your past. What has been a reoccurring theme through most of your experiences?

2. What are you passionate about?

3. What would you do if you knew you could not fail?

4. What does your future look like?

5. How can living on true purpose impact your life?

Study Guide #8

Welcome to Destiny

What is the definition of Expansion?

_____

_____

How does Expansion contribute to your character?

_____

_____

How does Expansion contribute to your F.R.E.E journey?

_____

_____

Fill in the Blank

You are _____ made.
You are _____ to conquer.
You are designed for _____.
You are here to _____.

Reflect the Light: John 8:12 "Then spake Jesus again unto them, saying, I am the light of the world. Whoever follows me will never walk in darkness, but will have the light of life.

What does it mean to have the light of life?
_____
_____

Group Discussion Questions:

1. How can you use life lessons to expand?

2. What steps can you take to make dreams and visions reality starting today?

3. How have you seen the affects of Expansion on your life? In what areas have you seen development?

4. How can you reflect development and Expansion to everyone you meet?

5. How can you counteract the roadblocks to your Expansion?

Study Guide #9

The Seven Benefits of Expansion

Name the Seven Benefits of Expansion

_____   _____

_____   _____

_____   _____

_____

How are the seven benefits contributing to your F.R.E.E journey?

_____

_____

Can you think of any additional benefits that you have seen during you journey?

_____

_____

Fill in the Blank:

God has made you uniquely and _____ to function in _____ from stereotypes and the standards of others. Your _____ is uniquely yours. Live this out as you journey and utilize the benefits of _____ to elevate you higher and higher.

Group Discussion Questions:

1. No two F.R.E.E journeys are alike, how can you fully embrace your unique journey?

2. What is the most prevalent of the Seven Benefits of Expansion you have seen in your life?

3. What benefit would you like to possess more of?

4. As defined determination is affirmation in action. How has your determination fueled your desire to pursue purpose?

5. How has gained from the benefit of wisdom (and knowledge) in your life?

Study Guide #10
Live New, Live F.R.E.E

Welcome to the F.R.E.E life. Being F.R.E.E is a life-long journey and there are ways to incorporate this liberation into your life daily. Living F.R.E.E impact your purpose, your passion and your character and truly changes you from the inside out.

What does awakening mean to you? Have you experienced an awakening?

_____
_____

How can you focus on more purpose and less on things that are not purpose-driven?

_____
_____

Name at least three ways from chapter ten to live F.R.E.E

_____
_____

Fill in the Blank

You are _____ for your life to be a display of God's blessings. Many people are broken, lost, without hope and wishing that someone would _____ them along on their difficult _____. You are _____ with a testimony of God's blessings to encourage, strengthen and inspire people. By _____ you assist others in reaching F.R.E.Edom.

Group Discussion Questions:

1. How can we walk boldly into God's promises?

2. What is the most effective way you can live F.R.E.E?

3. What has God given you in order to bless others?

4. How do you determine if an activity is meaningful and purpose-driven?

5. How can you make yourself available to be used purposefully?

Study Guide Answers

Study Guide #1:
F.R.E.E word answers: Finally, Release, Experience, Expansion

Fill in the Blanks answers: past, linked, experiences, valuable lessons, living.

Study Guide #2:
Fill in the Blank answers: timing, action, aspects, F.R.E.E, seize, effectively

Attributes of a Finally answers: Preparedness, Enablement, Awareness, Renewal

Study Guide # 3: (none)

Study Guide # 4:
Fill in the Blank answers: great work, solitary, necessary, renewed, strength, elevated, equipped

Study Guide #5: (none)

Study Guide #6: (none)

Study Guide #7:
Fill in the Blank: growth, growing, exist, dead, defines

Study Guide #8:
Fill in the Blank: purposefully, called, greatness, expand

Study Guide #9:
Benefits of Expansion: Clarity, Wisdom, Direction, Strength, Affirmation, Soundness of Mind and Wholeness

Fill in the Blank: complete, liberation, F.R.E.Edom, Expansion

Study Guide # 10:
Ways to Live F.R.E.E:
Share
Make an Impact
Move with Purpose
Set Goals
Anticipate an Attack
Dream Big
Strive for Greatness

Fill in the Blank: blessed, assist, journey, empowered, sharing

Made in the USA
Charleston, SC
15 February 2012